TOUCHING
ELEGANCE

TWENTY-ONE DESIGNS
BY
KIM HARGREAVES

CREDITS

DESIGNS & STYLING
Kim Hargreaves

EDITOR
Kathleen Hargreaves

HAIR & MAKE-UP
Diana Fisher

MODELS
Amanda & James Hare

PHOTOGRAPHY
Graham Watts

LAYOUTS
Angela Lin

PATTERNS
Sue Whiting & Trisha McKenzie

© Copyright Kim Hargreaves 2010
Published in 2010 by Kim Hargreaves
Intake Cottage, 26 Underbank Old Road, Holmfirth
West Yorkshire, HD9 1EA, England

British Library Cataloguing in Publication Data
A catalogue record for this book is available from the British Library

ISBN-10:   1 906487 08-9
ISBN-13:   978-1 906487 08-9

CONTENTS

As AUTUMN leaves fall...

Cross the threshold into a new season with an eclectic blend of chic sophistication and bohemian charm.

Warm tones of mulberry, chestnut and bitter chocolate sit beside a monochrome pallet of inky black and charcoal grey, drawing attention to the luscious yarns and sumptuous silhouettes.

FLORENCE — Timeless cardigan with many buttons

VIRGINIA — Belted jacket with shawl collar

DOLORES — Softly elegant shrug

PATSY — Neat cardigan with textured details

WILLIE — Waistcoat with shawl collar

RALPH — Understated button through sweater

BESSIE & JOSIE — Belted cardigan with pockets & snug textured hat (Opposite)

JOSIE — Neat textured hat

BESSIE & RALPH — Belted cardigan with pockets & button through sweater

ISADORA — A-line sweater with pockets & shaped front hem

VICTOR — Ribbed sweater with cuff detail

BETTY — Long-line random striped scarf

VICTOR, NELLIE & BOBBY — Rugged sweater, cosy raglan sweater & cabled scarf

WALLACE — Tailored jacket with buttoned pockets & cuffs

MAE — Understated vest with capped sleeves

RUTH — Cropped cabled sweater with buttoned detail

CARMEN — Chic jacket with side vents & crochet trims

NANCY — Long-line double breasted cardigan

ELEANOR — Sumptuous blousy sweater with graceful neckline

LOIS — Slouchy jacket with a touch of the bohemian

VICTOR — Rugged ribbed sweater

BOBBY & JOSIE — Long-line cabled scarf & cosy hat

VICTOR & LOIS — Ribbed sweater & slouchy jacket

BOBBY & JOSIE — Cabled scarf & snug textured hat

ELLA — Skimming sweater with softly draped neckline

MAE — Vest with capped sleeves

PATSY — Neat cardigan buttoned at the waist

THE PATTERNS

Recommendation

Suitable for the knitter with a little experience
Please see page 10 for photograph.

	XS-S	M-L	XL-XXL	
To fit	**81-86**	**91-97**	**102-109**	**cm**
bust	32-34	36-38	40-43	in

Rowan Cocoon

A Shale	4	5	5	x 100gm
B Crag	3	3	3	x 100gm
C Mountain	3	3	3	x 100gm
D Scree	3	3	3	x 100gm
E Alpine	3	3	3	x 100gm

Needles

1 pair 5mm (no 6) (US 8) needles
1 pair 5½mm (no 5) (US 9) needles
1 pair 6mm (no 4) (US 10) needles

Tension

16 sts and 20 rows to 10 cm measured over
patterned stocking stitch using 6mm (US 10)
needles.

VIRGINIA
JACKET WITH BELT & SHAWL COLLAR

BACK

Cast on 77 (85: 95) sts using 5mm (US 8)
needles and yarn A.
Beg with a K row, work in st st for 5 rows,
ending with a RS row.
Row 6 (WS): Knit (to form fold line).
Change to 6mm (US 10) needles.
Beg and ending rows as indicated and using
the **intarsia** method (see page 57), cont in patt
from chart for back and sleeves, which is worked
entirely in st st beg with a K row, as folls:
Work 26 (28: 28) rows, ending with a WS row.
Dec 1 st at each end of next and 2 foll 10th
rows. 71 (79: 89) sts.
Work 19 rows, ending with a WS row.
Inc 1 st at each end of next and 2 foll 10th
rows. 77 (85: 95) sts.
Work 11 rows, ending after chart row 98
(100: 100) and with a WS row. (Back should
measure 49 (50: 50) cm from fold line row.)
Shape armholes
Keeping patt correct, cast off 3 (4: 4) sts at
beg of next 2 rows. 71 (77: 87) sts.
Dec 1 st at each end of next 5 (5: 7) rows,
then on foll 2 (3: 3) alt rows, then on foll 4th
row. 55 (59: 65) sts.
Cont straight until chart row 136 (140: 144)
has been completed, ending with a WS row.
(Armhole should measure 19 (20: 22) cm.)
Shape shoulders and back neck
Cast off 5 (5: 6) sts at beg of next 2 rows.
45 (49: 53) sts.
Next row (RS): Cast off 5 sts, patt until there
are 7 (8: 8) sts on right needle and turn,
leaving rem sts on a holder.
Work each side of neck separately.
Cast off 3 sts at beg of next row.
Cast off rem 4 (5: 5) sts.
With RS facing, rejoin yarns to rem sts, cast
off centre 21 (23: 27) sts, patt to end.
Complete to match first side, reversing
shapings.

LEFT FRONT

Cast on 46 (50: 55) sts using 5mm (US 8)
needles and yarn A.
Beg with a K row, work in st st as folls:
Work 1 row, ending with a RS row.
Inc 1 st at beg of next row and at same edge on
foll 3 rows, ending with a RS row. 50 (54: 59) sts.

Row 6 (WS): Knit (to form fold line).
Change to 6mm (US 10) needles.
Beg and ending rows as indicated and using
the **intarsia** method, cont in patt from chart
for back and sleeves, which is worked entirely
in st st beg with a K row, as folls:
Work 26 (28: 28) rows, ending with a WS row.
Dec 1 st at beg of next and 2 foll 10th rows.
47 (51: 56) sts.
Work 17 (15: 15) rows, ending with a WS row.
Now working in patt from chart for upper
fronts, cont as folls:
Work 2 rows, ending with a WS row.
Shape for collar
Inc 1 st at end of next and foll 14 alt rows,
then on 0 (1: 1) foll 4th row **and at same time**
inc 1 st at beg of next (3rd: 3rd) and 2 foll
10th rows.
65 (70: 75) sts.
Work 3 (1: 1) rows, ending after chart row
98 (100: 100) and with a WS row.
Shape armhole
Keeping patt correct, cast off 3 (4: 4) sts at
beg and inc 1 (0: 0) st at end of next row.
63 (66: 71) sts.
Work 1 row.
Dec 1 st at armhole edge of next 5 (5: 7) rows,
then on foll 2 (3: 3) alt rows, then on foll 4th
row **and at same time** inc 1 st at end of 3rd
(next: next) and 2 (3: 4) foll 4th rows.
58 (61: 65) sts.
Inc 1 st at front opening edge only on 2nd
(2nd: 4th) and 5 foll 4th rows.
64 (67: 71) sts.
Work 1 row, ending after chart row 136 (140:
144) and with a WS row.
Shape shoulder
Cast off 5 (5: 6) sts at beg of next row, 5 sts at
beg of foll alt row, then 4 (5: 5) sts at beg of
foll alt row **and at same time** inc 1 (1: 0) st at
front opening edge of 3rd of these rows.
51 (53: 55) sts.
Size XS-S only
Inc 1 st at front opening edge of 2nd row.
52 sts.
All sizes
Cont as set for a further 15 (14: 12) rows (for
back collar extension), ending with a WS (**RS:
RS**) row.
Cast off in patt.

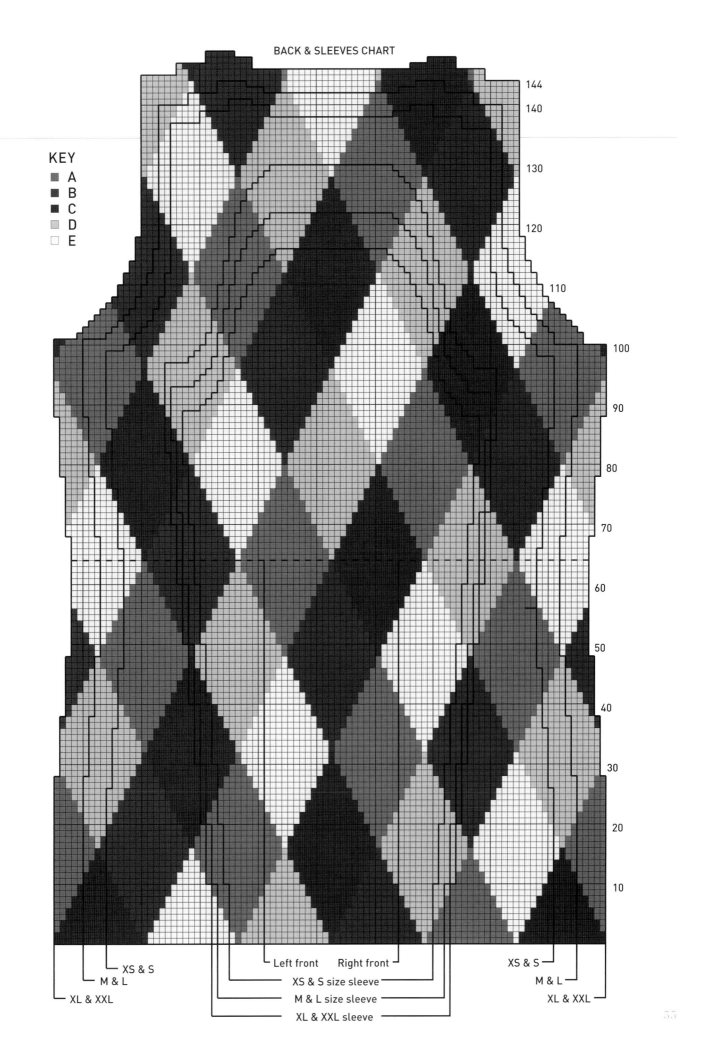

BACK & SLEEVES CHART

KEY
A
B
C
D
E

144
140
130
120
110
100
90
80
70
60
50
40
30
20
10

XS & S
M & L
XL & XXL

Left front   Right front
XS & S size sleeve
M & L size sleeve
XL & XXL sleeve

XS & S
M & L
XL & XXL

RIGHT FRONT

Cast on 46 (50: 55) sts using 5mm (US 8) needles and yarn A.

Beg with a K row, work in st st as folls:

Work 1 row, ending with a RS row.

Inc 1 st at end of next row and at same edge on foll 3 rows, ending with a RS row. 50 (54: 59) sts.

Row 6 (WS): Knit (to form fold line).

Change to 6mm (US 10) needles.

Beg and ending rows as indicated and using the **intarsia** method, cont in patt from chart for back and sleeves, which is worked entirely in st st beg with a K row, as folls:

Work 26 (28: 28) rows, ending with a WS row.

Dec 1 st at end of next and 2 foll 10th rows. 47 (51: 56) sts.

Complete to match left front, reversing shapings.

SLEEVES (both alike)

Cast on 35 (39: 41) sts using 5mm (US 8) needles and yarn A.

Beg with a K row, work in st st for 5 rows, ending with a RS row.

Row 6 (WS): Knit (to form fold line).

Change to 6mm (US 10) needles.

Beg and ending rows as indicated and using the **intarsia** method, cont in patt from chart for back and sleeves, which is worked entirely in st st beg with a K row, as folls:

Work 10 rows, ending with a WS row.

Inc 1 st at each end of next and 7 (5: 5) foll 10th rows, then on 0 (2: 2) foll 12th rows, taking inc sts into patt. 51 (55: 57) sts.

Work 7 (7: 11) rows, ending after chart row 88 (92: 96) and with a WS row.

(Sleeve should measure 44 (46: 48) cm from fold line row.)

Shape top

Keeping patt correct, cast off 3 (4: 4) sts at beg of next 2 rows. 45 (47: 49) sts.

Dec 1 st at each end of next 3 rows, then on foll alt row, then on 3 (4: 5) foll 4th rows. 31 sts.

Work 1 row, ending with a WS row.

Dec 1 st at each end of next and foll 2 (1: 1) alt rows, then on foll 3 rows, ending with a WS row.

Cast off rem 19 (21: 21) sts.

MAKING UP

Pin the pieces out and steam gently without allowing the iron to touch the yarn.

Join both shoulder seams using back stitch or mattress stitch if preferred. Join cast-off edges of back collar extensions, then sew one edge to back neck.

Left front facing

With RS facing, using 5mm (US 8) needles and yarn A, beg at first collar increase, pick up and knit 50 sts evenly down left front opening edge to fold line row.

Row 1 (WS): Knit (to form fold line).

Row 2: Cast on 2 sts, K to last 2 sts, K2tog. 51 sts.

Row 3: P to last st, inc in last st. 52 sts.

Rep last 2 rows twice more, ending with a WS row. 56 sts.

Cast off.

Right front facing

With RS facing, using 5mm (US 8) needles and yarn A, beg at fold line row, pick up and knit 50 sts evenly up right front opening edge to first collar increase.

Row 1 (WS): Knit (to form fold line).

Row 2: K2tog, K to last st, inc in last st. 50 sts.

Row 3: Cast on 2 sts, P to end. 52 sts.

Rep last 2 rows twice more, ending with a WS row. 56 sts.

Cast off.

Join side seams. Join sleeve seams. Insert sleeves into armholes. At lower edges of fronts, join shaped row-end edges of front facing and first 5 rows of fronts to form mitred corner. Fold front facings and first 5 rows of back and fronts to inside along fold line rows and neatly sew in place. Fold collar in half to inside so that outer row-end edge matches back neck seam, then neatly sew in place, joining collar to top shaped row-end edge of front facings. Around lower edge of sleeves, fold first 5 rows to inside along fold line row and neatly sew in place.

Belt

Cast on 15 sts using 5½mm (US 9) needles and yarn C.

Beg and ending rows as indicated and using the **intarsia** method, cont in patt from chart for belt, which is worked entirely in st st beg with a K row, as folls:

Rep the 50 row patt rep until belt measures 160 (170: 180) cm, ending with a WS row.

Cast off.

Join row-end edges of belt to form a long tube, then sew ends closed.

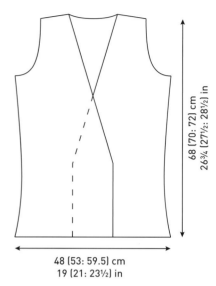

68 (70: 72) cm
26¾ (27½: 28½) in

48 (53: 59.5) cm
19 (21: 23½) in

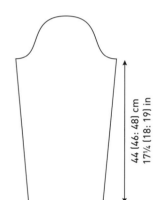

44 (46: 48) cm
17¼ (18: 19) in

BELT CHART

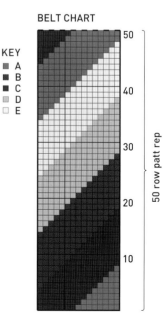

KEY
- A
- B
- C
- D
- E

50 row patt rep

UPPER FRONTS CHART

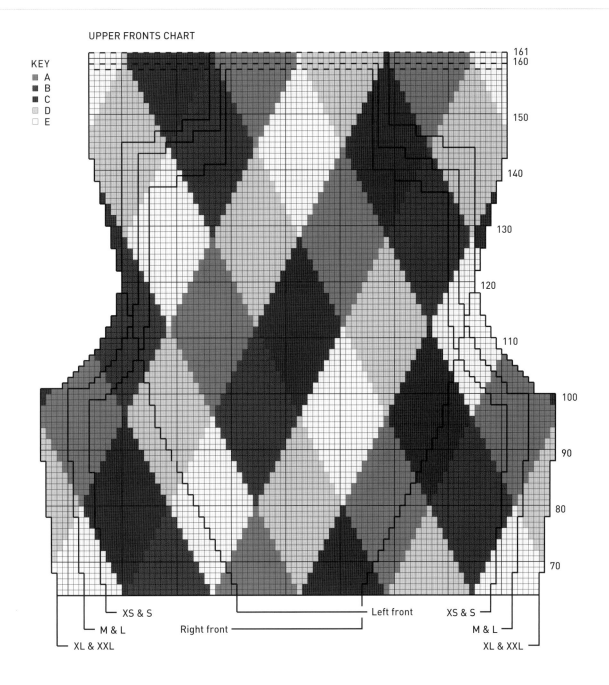

KEY
- A
- B
- C
- D
- E

161
160
150
140
130
120
110
100
90
80
70

XS & S — Left front — XS & S
M & L — Right front — M & L
XL & XXL — XL & XXL

INTARSIA TECHNIQUE

The intarsia method of knitting produces a single thickness of fabric and is used where a colour is only required in a particular area of a row. Use short lengths of yarn for each block of colour, then joining in the different colours at the appropriate point on the row, link one colour to the next by twisting them around each other where they meet on the wrong side to avoid gaps. Ends can then be darned along the colour join lines, as each motif is completed.

Recommendation

Suitable for the knitter with a little experience
Please see pages 48 & 49 for photographs.

	XS	S	M	L	XL	XXL	
To fit	**81**	**86**	**91**	**97**	**102**	**109**	cm
bust	32	34	36	38	40	43	in

Rowan Kidsilk Haze

| | 5 | 5 | 6 | 6 | 7 | 7 | x 25gm |

Photographed in Anthracite

Needles

1 pair 3¼mm (no 10) (US 3) needles

Tension

25 sts and 34 rows to 10 cm measured over
stocking stitch using 3¼mm (US 3) needles.

ELLA
SKIMMING SWEATER WITH SOFTLY DRAPED NECKLINE

BACK

Cast on 224 (236: 248: 260: 272: 292) sts
using 3¼mm (US 3) needles.

Row 1 (RS): *K2, lift 2nd st on right needle
over first st and off right needle, rep from
* to end.

112 (118: 124: 130: 136: 146) sts.

Beg with a P row, work in st for 29 rows,
ending with a WS row.

Row 31 (dec) (RS): K3, K2tog, K to last 5 sts,
K2tog tbl, K3.

Working all side seam decreases as set by
last row, dec 1 st at each end of 10th and
4 foll 10th rows.

100 (106: 112: 118: 124: 134) sts.

Work 27 rows, ending with a WS row.

Next row (inc) (RS): K3, M1, K to last 3 sts,
M1, K3.

Working all side seam increases as set by
last row, inc 1 st at each end of 12th and
2 foll 12th rows.

108 (114: 120: 126: 132: 142) sts.

Cont straight until back measures
47 (47: 48: 48: 48: 48) cm, ending
with a WS row.

Shape armholes

Cast off 4 (5: 5: 6: 6: 7) sts at beg of next
2 rows.

100 (104: 110: 114: 120: 128) sts.

Dec 1 st at each end of next 5 (5: 7: 7: 9: 9)
rows, then on foll 3 (4: 4: 4: 4: 7) alt rows,
then on 2 foll 4th rows.

80 (82: 84: 88: 90: 92) sts.

Cont straight until armhole measures
17 (18: 18: 19: 20: 21) cm, ending
with a WS row.

Place blue markers at both ends of last row.

Shape shoulders

Cast off 7 (7: 7: 8: 8: 9) sts at beg of next
2 rows, then 7 (7: 8: 8: 9: 9) sts at beg of
foll 2 rows.

Cast off rem 52 (54: 54: 56: 56: 56) sts
loosely.

Place red markers at both ends of final
cast-off edge.

FRONT

Work as given for back until 34 rows less have
been worked than on back to beg of shoulder
shaping, ending with a WS row.

Shape for cowl neck

Inc 1 st at each end of next and foll 15 alt
rows.

112 (114: 116: 120: 122: 124) sts.

Place blue markers at both ends of last row.

Work 19 (19: 21: 21: 23: 25) rows, ending
with a WS row.

Place red markers at both ends of last row.

Work 20 (20: 22: 22: 24: 26) rows, ending
with a WS row.

Dec 1 st at each end of next and foll 6 alt rows.

Work 1 row, ending with a WS row.

Cast off rem 98 (100: 102: 106: 108: 110) sts
loosely.

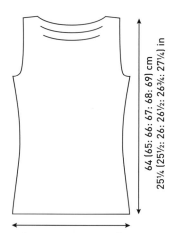

64 (65: 66: 67: 68: 69) cm
25¼ (25½: 26: 26½: 26¾: 27¼) in

43 (45.5: 48: 50.5: 53: 57) cm
17 (18: 19: 20: 21: 22½) in

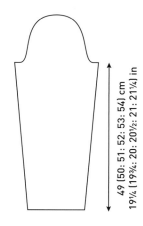

49 (50: 51: 52: 53: 54) cm
19¼ (19¾: 20: 20½: 21: 21¼) in

Continued on next page...

Recommendation

Suitable for the novice knitter
Please see pages 23, 45 & 46 for photographs.

One size

Rowan Big Wool or Drift

1 x 100gm

Photographed in Mulberry & Smokey Big Wool
and Wanderer Drift

Needles

1 pair 10mm (no 000) (US 15) needles

Tension

10 sts and 13 rows to 10 cm measured over
stocking stitch using 10mm (US 15) needles.

JOSIE
NEAT FITTING TEXTURED HAT

HAT
Cast on 41 sts using 10mm (US 15) needles.
Rows 1 to 8: Purl.
Row 9 (RS): Knit.
Row 10: Purl.
Rows 11 and 12: Knit.
Rows 13 and 14: Purl.
Rows 15 to 20: As rows 9 to 14.
Beg with a K row, complete hat in st st
as folls:
Work 4 rows, ending with a WS row.
Shape top
Row 1 (RS): (K3, K2tog) 8 times, K1.
33 sts.
Work 3 rows.
Row 5: (K2, K2tog) 8 times, K1. 25 sts.
Work 1 row.
Row 7: (K1, K2tog) 8 times, K1. 17 sts.
Row 8: P1, (P2tog) 8 times.
Break yarn and thread through rem 9 sts.
Pull up tight and fasten off securely.

MAKING UP
Join back seam, preferably using mattress
stitch.

Ella – Continued from previous page...

SLEEVES
Cast on 94 (98: 102: 110: 114: 118) sts using
3¼mm (US 3) needles.
Row 1 (RS): *K2, lift 2nd st on right needle
over first st and off right needle, rep from
* to end. 47 (49: 51: 55: 57: 59) sts.
Beg with a P row, work in st for 29 rows,
ending with a WS row.
Working all sleeve increases in same way as side
seam increases, inc 1 st at each end of next and
every foll 10th (8th: 10th: 10th: 10th: 10th) row
to 73 (57: 71: 71: 69: 81) sts, then on every foll
– (10th: 12th: 12th: 12th: 12th) row until there
are - (77: 77: 81: 83: 87) sts.

Cont straight until sleeve measures 49 (50:
51: 52: 53: 54) cm, ending with a WS row.
Shape top
Cast off 4 (5: 5: 6: 6: 7) sts at beg of next
2 rows.
65 (67: 67: 69: 71: 73) sts.
Dec 1 st at each end of next 3 rows, then
on foll alt row, then on 7 foll 4th rows.
43 (45: 45: 47: 49: 51) sts.
Work 1 row, ending with a WS row.
Dec 1 st at each end of next and every foll alt
row to 39 sts, then on foll 7 rows, ending with
a WS row.
Cast off rem 25 sts.

MAKING UP
Pin the pieces out and steam gently without
allowing the iron to touch the yarn.
Join shoulder seams between red and blue
markers, using back stitch or mattress stitch if
preferred. Fold cowl section to inside level with
red markers and neatly sew row-end edges in
place to seams on inside.
Join side seams. Join sleeve seams. Insert
sleeves into armholes.

Recommendation

Suitable for the knitter with a little experience
Please see pages 12, 13 & 51 for photographs.

	XS	S	M	L	XL	XXL	
To fit	**81**	**86**	**91**	**97**	**102**	**109**	cm
bust	32	34	36	38	40	43	in

Rowan Felted Tweed

	5	5	6	6	7	7	x 50gm

Photographed in Duck Egg

Rowan Wool Cotton

	7	8	8	9	9	10	x 50gm

Photographed in Inky

Needles

1 pair 3mm (no 11) (US 2/3) needles
1 pair 3¾mm (no 9) (US 5) needles

Buttons - 5

Tension

23 sts and 32 rows to 10 cm measured over
stocking stitch using 3¾mm (US 5) needles.

Special abbreviations

MP = make picot as folls: cast on 1 st, cast off
1 st – one st on right needle.

PATSY
NEAT FITTING CARDIGAN BUTTONED AT THE WAIST

BACK

Cast on 74 (80: 86: 92: 98: 106) sts using
3mm (US 2/3) needles.
Row 1 (RS): K0 (0: 0: 1: 0: 0), P2 (1: 0: 2: 2:
2), *K2, P2, rep from * to last 0 (3: 2: 1: 0: 0)
sts, K0 (2: 2: 1: 0: 0), P0 (1: 0: 0: 0: 0).
Row 2: P0 (0: 0: 1: 0: 0), K2 (1: 0: 2: 2: 2),
*P2, K2, rep from * to last 0 (3: 2: 1: 0: 0) sts,
P0 (2: 2: 1: 0: 0), K0 (1: 0: 0: 0: 0).
These 2 rows form rib.
Work in rib for a further 33 rows, ending with
a **RS** row.
Row 36 (WS): Rib 13 (14: 15: 16: 17: 17),
M1, *rib 24 (26: 28: 30: 32: 36), M1, rep
from * once more, rib 13 (14: 15: 16: 17: 17).
77 (83: 89: 95: 101: 109) sts.
Change to 3¾mm (US 5) needles.
Now work in patt as folls:
Row 1 (RS): Knit.
Row 2: Purl.
Row 3: K2, M1, K to last 2 sts, M1, K2.
79 (85: 91: 97: 103: 111) sts.
Row 4: Purl.
Rows 5 to 10: As rows 1 and 2, 3 times.
Row 11: As row 3. 81 (87: 93: 99: 105: 113) sts.
Row 12: K1 (0: 1: 0: 1: 1), *P1, K1, rep from *
to last 0 (1: 0: 1: 0: 0) st, P0 (1: 0: 1: 0: 0).
Rows 13 and 14: As row 12.
These 14 rows form patt (of 11 rows in st st
followed by 3 rows of moss st) and beg side
seam shaping.
Working all side seam increases as set by row
3, cont in patt, shaping side seams by inc 1 st
at each end of 5th and 3 foll 10th rows, taking
inc sts into patt. 89 (95: 101: 107: 113: 121) sts.
Work 9 (9: 13: 13: 13: 13) rows, ending with
a WS row.

Shape armholes

Keeping patt correct, cast off 3 (4: 4: 5: 5: 6)
sts at beg of next 2 rows.
83 (87: 93: 97: 103: 109) sts.
Dec 1 st at each end of next 5 (5: 7: 7: 9: 9)
rows, then on foll 1 (2: 2: 3: 3: 4) alt rows, then
on foll 4th row. 69 (71: 73: 75: 77: 81) sts.
Cont straight until all 14 patt rows have been
worked 7 times in total, ending with a WS row.
Now cont in moss st **throughout** (as set by
patt rows 12 to 14) until armhole measures
17 (18: 18: 19: 20: 21) cm, ending with
a WS row.

Shape shoulders and back neck

Cast off 7 (7: 7: 7: 7: 8) sts at beg of next
2 rows. 55 (57: 59: 61: 63: 65) sts.
Next row (RS): Cast off 7 (7: 7: 7: 7: 8) sts,
moss st until there are 10 (10: 11: 11: 12: 12)
sts on right needle and turn, leaving rem sts
on a holder.
Work each side of neck separately.
Cast off 4 sts at beg of next row.
Cast off rem 6 (6: 7: 7: 8: 8) sts.
With RS facing, rejoin yarn to rem sts, cast
off centre 21 (23: 23: 25: 25: 25) sts, moss
st to end.
Complete to match first side, reversing shapings.

LEFT FRONT

Cast on 43 (46: 49: 52: 55: 59) sts using
3mm (US 2/3) needles.
Row 1 (RS): K0 (0: 0: 1: 0: 0), P2 (1: 0: 2: 2:
2), *K2, P2, rep from * to last 5 sts, K5.
Row 2: MP, K until there are 7 sts on right
needle, *P2, K2, rep from * to last 0 (3: 2: 1:
0: 0) sts, P0 (2: 2: 1: 0: 0), K0 (1: 0: 0: 0: 0).
Row 3: As row 1.
Row 4: K7, *P2, K2, rep from * to last 0 (3: 2: 1:
0: 0) sts, P0 (2: 2: 1: 0: 0), K0 (1: 0: 0: 0: 0).
These 2 rows set the sts – front opening edge
5 sts in g st with picot worked on every 4th
row and all other sts in rib.
Cont as set for a further 32 rows, ending with
a WS row.
Change to 3¾mm (US 5) needles.
Now work in patt as folls:
Row 1 (RS): Knit.
Row 2: Patt until there are 5 sts on right
needle, P to end.

Shape front slope

Row 3: K2, M1, K to last 7 sts, K2tog tbl, K5.
43 (46: 49: 52: 55: 59) sts.
Row 4: Patt until there are 5 sts on right
needle, P to end.
Rows 5 to 8: As rows 1 and 2, twice.
Row 9: K to last 7 sts, K2tog tbl, K5.
42 (45: 48: 51: 54: 58) sts.
Row 10: As row 2.
Row 11: K2, M1, K to end.
43 (46: 49: 52: 55: 59) sts.
Row 12: Patt until there are 5 sts on right
needle, *P1, K1, rep from * to last 0 (1: 0: 1: 0:
0) st, P0 (1: 0: 1: 0: 0).

Row 13: K1 (0: 1: 0: 1: 1), *P1, K1, rep from * to last 6 sts, P1, K5.

Row 14: As row 12.

These 14 rows form patt (of 11 rows in st st followed by 3 rows of moss st) and beg side seam and front slope shaping.

Working all side seam increases and all front slope decreases as set by row 3, cont in patt as folls:

Dec 1 st at front slope edge of next and 4 (6: 4: 7: 5: 3) foll 6th rows, then on 2 (0: 2: 0: 2: 3) foll 8th rows **and at same time** inc 1 st at side seam edge of 5th and 3 foll 10th rows. 40 (43: 46: 48: 51: 56) sts.

Work 3 (7: 7: 5: 1: 5) rows, ending with a WS row.

Shape armhole

Keeping patt correct, cast off 3 (4: 4: 5: 5: 6) sts at beg and dec 0 (1: 1: 0: 0: 0) st at front slope edge of next row. 37 (38: 41: 43: 46: 50) sts. Work 1 row.

Dec 1 st at armhole edge of next 5 (5: 7: 7: 9: 9) rows, then on foll 1 (2: 2: 3: 3: 4) alt rows, then on foll 4th row **and at same time** dec 1 st at front slope edge of 3rd (7th: 7th: next: 5th: next) and 1 (0: 1: 2: 1: 2) foll 8th rows. 28 (29: 29: 29: 31: 33) sts.

Working all 14 patt rows 7 times in total and then completing left front in moss st (keeping front opening edge 5 sts in patt as set), cont as folls:

Dec 1 st at front slope edge **only** on 8th (2nd: 8th: 8th: 2nd: 4th) and 1 (2: 1: 1: 2: 2) foll 8th rows, then on foll 10th row. 25 (25: 26: 26: 27: 29) sts.

Cont straight until left front matches back to beg of shoulder shaping, ending with a WS row.

Shape shoulder

Cast off 7 (7: 7: 7: 7: 8) sts at beg of next and for alt row, then 6 (6: 7: 7: 8: 8) sts at beg of foll alt row.

Cont as set on rem 5 sts only for a further 6 (6.5: 6.5: 7: 7: 7) cm (for back neck border extension), ending with a WS row. Cast off.

RIGHT FRONT

Cast on 43 (46: 49: 52: 55: 59) sts using 3mm (US 2/3) needles.

Row 1 (RS): MP, K until there are 5 sts on right needle, P2, *K2, P2, rep from * to last 0 (3: 2: 1: 0: 0) sts, K0 (2: 2: 1: 0: 0), P0 (1: 0: 0: 0: 0).

Row 2: P0 (0: 0: 1: 0: 0), K2 (1: 0: 2: 2: 2), *P2, K2, rep from * to last 5 sts, K5.

Row 3: K5, P2, *K2, P2, rep from * to last 0 (3: 2: 1: 0: 0) sts, K0 (2: 2: 1: 0: 0), P0 (1: 0: 0: 0: 0).

Row 4: As row 2.

These 2 rows set the sts – front opening edge 5 sts in g st with picot worked on every 4th row and all other sts in rib.

Keeping sts correct as now set, cont as folls:

Row 5 (buttonhole row) (RS): Patt until there is 1 st on right needle, K2tog, yfwd (to make a buttonhole), patt to end.

Work 7 rows.

Rep last 8 rows 3 times more, ending with a WS row.

Change to 3¾mm (US 5) needles.

Now work in patt as folls:

Row 1 (RS): Patt until there is 1 st on right needle, K2tog, yfwd (to make 5th buttonhole), K to end.

Row 2: P to last 5 sts, K5.

Shape front slope

Row 3: Patt until there are 5 sts on right needle, K2tog, K to last 2 sts, M1, K2. 43 (46: 49: 52: 55: 59) sts.

Last 3 rows set the sts.

Keeping patt correct as now set and working all increases and decreases as set by last row, complete to match left front, rev shapings.

SLEEVES

Main section

Cast on 77 (81: 81: 85: 87: 91) sts using 3¾mm (US 5) needles.

Work in patt as folls:

Row 1 (RS): Knit.

Row 2: Purl.

Rows 3 to 6: As rows 1 and 2, twice.

Row 7: K2, K2tog, K to last 4 sts, K2tog tbl, K2. 75 (79: 79: 83: 85: 89) sts.

Row 8: Purl.

Row 9: Knit.

Row 10: P1, *K1, P1, rep from * to end.

Rows 11 and 12: As row 10.

Row 13: As row 7. 73 (77: 77: 81: 83: 87) sts.

Row 14: Purl.

These 14 rows form patt (of 11 rows in st st followed by 3 rows of moss st) and beg sleeve shaping.

Working all decreases as set by row 7, cont in patt as folls:

Dec 1 st at each end of 5th and foll 8th row, then on foll 16th row. 67 (71: 71: 75: 77: 81) sts.

Cont straight until sleeve measures approx 22 (22: 23: 23: 23: 23) cm, ending after same patt row as on back to beg of armhole shaping and with a WS row.

Shape top

Keeping patt correct, cast off 3 (4: 4: 5: 5: 6) sts at beg of next 2 rows. 61 (63: 63: 65: 67: 69) sts.

Dec 1 st at each end of next 3 rows, then on foll alt row, then on 6 foll 4th rows. 41 (43: 43: 45: 47: 49) sts.

Work 1 row, ending with a WS row.

Dec 1 st at each end of next and every foll alt row to 37 sts, then on foll 5 rows, ending with a WS row. Cast off rem 27 sts.

Cuff

With RS facing and using 3mm (US 2/3) needles, pick up and knit 77 (81: 81: 85: 87: 91) sts along cast-on edge of main section.

Row 1 (WS): P4 (6: 6: 8: 6: 8), P2tog, (P1, P2tog) 22 (22: 22: 22: 24: 24) times, P5 (7: 7: 9: 7: 9). 54 (58: 58: 62: 62: 66) sts.

Row 2: P2, *K2, P2, rep from * to end.

Row 3: K2, *P2, K2, rep from * to end.

Last 2 rows form rib.

Cont in rib, dec 1 st at each end of 9th and foll 10th row. 50 (54: 54: 58: 58: 62) sts.

Cont straight until cuff measures 10 cm from pick-up row, ending with a WS row. Cast off in rib.

MAKING UP

Pin the pieces out and steam gently without allowing the iron to touch the yarn.

Join shoulder seams using back stitch or mattress stitch if preferred. Join cast-off ends of back neck border extensions, then sew one edge to back neck edge. Join side seams. Join sleeve seams. Insert sleeves into armholes. Sew on buttons.

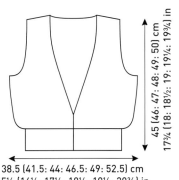

38.5 (41.5: 44: 46.5: 49: 52.5) cm
15¼ (16¼: 17¼: 18¼: 19¼: 20¾) in

45 (46: 47: 48: 49: 50) cm
17¾ (18: 18½: 19: 19¼: 19¾) in

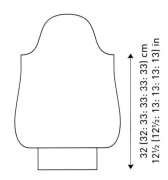

32 (32: 33: 33: 33: 33) cm
12½ (12½: 13: 13: 13: 13) in

Recommendation

Suitable for the knitter with a little experience
Please see pages 16 & 17 for photographs.

	XS	S	M	L	XL	XXL	
To fit	**81**	**86**	**91**	**97**	**102**	**109**	cm
bust	32	34	36	38	40	43	in

Rowan Felted Tweed

| | 5 | 5 | 6 | 6 | 6 | 7 | x 50gm |
Photographed in Treacle

Needles

1 pair 3¾mm (no 9) (US 5) needles

Tension

24 sts and 39 rows to 10 cm measured over
moss stitch using 3¾mm (US 5) needles.

Pattern note: As there are no edgings added
afterwards, front opening and armhole row-
end edges form actual finished edges of
garment. To ensure these edges remain neat,
try to join in new balls of yarn along side seam
edges only.

WILLIE
WAISTCOAT WORKED IN MOSS STITCH WITH SHAWL COLLAR

BACK

Cast on 85 (91: 97: 103: 109: 119) sts using
3¾mm (US 5) needles.
Row 1 (RS): K1, P1, K1, wrap next st (by
slipping next st on left needle onto right
needle, taking yarn to opposite side of work
between needles and then slipping same st
back onto left needle – when working back
across wrapped sts, work the wrapped st and
the wrapping loop tog as one st) and turn.
Row 2: K1, P1, K1.
Row 3: (K1, P1) 3 times, wrap next st and turn.
Row 4: (P1, K1) 3 times.
Row 5: (K1, P1) 4 times, K1, wrap next st and
turn.
Row 6: K1, (P1, K1) 4 times.
These 6 rows set position of moss st.
Keeping moss st correct as now set, cont
as folls:
Row 7: Moss st 12 sts, wrap next st and turn.
Row 8: Moss st to end.
Row 9: Moss st 16 sts, wrap next st and turn.
Row 10: Moss st to end.
Row 11: Moss st 20 sts, wrap next st and turn.
Row 12: Moss st to end.
Row 13: Moss st 24 sts, wrap next st and turn.
Row 14: Moss st to end.
Row 15: Moss st 29 sts, wrap next st and turn.
Row 16: Moss st to end.
Row 17: Moss st 35 sts, wrap next st and turn.
Row 18: Moss st to end.
Row 19: Moss st across all sts.
Now rep rows 1 to 18 again.
Row 38: Moss st across all sts.
Cont in moss st for 10 (10: 14: 14: 14: 14)
rows, ending with a WS row.
Next row (inc) (RS): Moss st 3 sts, (K1, P1,
K1) all into next st – 2 sts increased, moss st
to last 4 sts, (K1, P1, K1) all into next st – 2 sts
increased, moss st 3 sts.
Working all increases as set by last row, inc
2 sts at each end of 30th and foll 30th row.
97 (103: 109: 115: 121: 131) sts.
Work 27 rows, ending with a WS row. (Back
should measure 30 (30: 31: 31: 31: 31) cm
along side seam edge.)
Shape armholes
Keeping moss st correct, cast off 4 (6: 6: 8:
9: 9) sts at beg of next 2 rows.
89 (91: 97: 99: 103: 113) sts.

Next row (dec) (RS): Moss st 3 sts, work 3 tog,
moss st to last 6 sts, work 3 tog, moss st 3 sts.
Working all armhole decrease as set by last
row, dec 2 sts at each end of 2nd and foll 2 (2:
3: 3: 3: 4) alt rows, then on 2 (2: 2: 2: 2: 3)
foll 4th rows. 65 (67: 69: 71: 75: 77) sts.
Work 35 (39: 37: 41: 45: 43) rows, ending
with a WS row.
Working armhole increases in same way as
side seam increases, inc 2 sts at each end of
next and foll 12th row, then on foll 10th row.
77 (79: 81: 83: 87: 89) sts.
Work 5 rows, ending with a WS row.
Shape back neck
Next row (RS): Moss st 24 (24: 25: 25: 27:
28) sts and turn, leaving rem sts on a holder.
Work each side of neck separately.
Dec 1 st at neck edge of next row.
23 (23: 24: 24: 26: 27) sts.
Shape shoulder
Cast off 7 (7: 7: 7: 8: 8) sts at beg and dec
1 st at end of next row.
Work 1 row.
Rep last 2 rows once more.
Cast off rem 7 (7: 8: 8: 8: 9) sts.
With RS facing, rejoin yarn to rem sts, cast
off centre 29 (31: 31: 33: 33: 33) sts, moss
st to end.
Complete to match first side, rev shapings.

LEFT FRONT

Cast on 69 (72: 75: 78: 81: 86) sts **quite
loosely** using 3¾mm (US 5) needles.
Row 1 (RS): *K1, P1, rep from * to last 1 (0: 1:
0: 1: 0) st, K1 (0: 1: 0: 1: 0).
This row sets position on moss st as given
for back.
Keeping moss st correct, cont as folls:
Row 2: Moss st 5 (5: 6: 6: 6: 7) sts, wrap
next st and turn.
Row 3: Moss st to end.
Row 4: Moss st 10 (10: 12: 12: 12: 14) sts,
wrap next st and turn.
Row 5: Moss st to end.
Row 6: Moss st 14 (15: 17: 18: 18: 20) sts,
wrap next st and turn.
Row 7: Moss st to end.
Row 8: Moss st 18 (20: 22: 23: 24: 26) sts,
wrap next st and turn.
Row 9: Moss st to end.

Row 10: Moss st 22 (24: 27: 28: 29: 32) sts, wrap next st and turn.
Row 11: Moss st to end.
Row 12: Moss st 26 (28: 31: 33: 34: 37) sts, wrap next st and turn.
Row 13: Moss st to end.
Row 14: Moss st 29 (32: 35: 37: 39: 42) sts, wrap next st and turn.
Row 15: Moss st to end.
Row 16: Moss st 32 (35: 38: 41: 43: 47) sts, wrap next st and turn.
Row 17: Moss st to end.
Row 18: Moss st 35 (38: 41: 44: 47: 51) sts, wrap next st and turn.
Row 19: Moss st to end.
Row 20: Moss st 38 (41: 44: 47: 50: 55) sts, wrap next st and turn.
Row 21: Moss st to end.
Row 22: Moss st to last 28 sts, wrap next st and turn.
Row 23: Moss st to end.
Row 24: Moss st to last 25 sts, wrap next st and turn.
Row 25: Moss st to end.
Row 26: Moss st to last 22 sts, wrap next st and turn.
Row 27: Moss st to end.
Row 28: Moss st to last 19 sts, wrap next st and turn.
Row 29: Moss st to end.
Row 30: Moss st to last 16 sts, wrap next st and turn.
Row 31: Moss st to end.
Row 32: Moss st to last 13 sts, wrap next st and turn.
Row 33: Moss st to end.
Row 34: Moss st to last 10 sts, wrap next st and turn.
Row 35: Moss st to end.
Row 36: Moss st to last 8 sts, wrap next st and turn.
Row 37: Moss st to end.
Row 38: Moss st to last 6 sts, wrap next st and turn.
Row 39: Moss st to end.
Row 40: Moss st to last 4 sts, wrap next st and turn.
Row 41: Moss st to end.
Row 42: Moss st to last 2 sts, wrap next st and turn.
Row 43: Moss st to end.
Row 44: Moss st across all sts.
Cont in moss st for 24 (24: 28: 28: 28: 28) rows, ending with a WS row.
Working all front opening edge increases in same way as back side seam increases and all front side seam decreases in same way

as back armhole decreases, cont as folls:
Inc 2 sts at end of next and foll 10th row, then on 2 foll 8th rows, then on foll 6th row **and at same time** dec 2 sts at beg of 5th row. 77 (80: 83: 86: 89: 94) sts.
Dec 2 sts at side seam edge of 2nd and foll 30th row. 73 (76: 79: 82: 85: 90) sts.
Work 1 row, ending with a WS row.

Shape front slope
Next row (RS): Moss st to last 25 (26: 26: 27: 27: 27) sts, work 3 tog, moss st to end.
Working all front slope decreases as set by last row, dec 2 sts at front opening edge of 8th (8th: 8th: 10th: 10th: 10th) and 2 (1: 1: 1: 1: 1) foll 8th (10th: 10th: 10th: 10th: 10th) rows. 65 (70: 73: 76: 79: 84) sts.
Work 1 (7: 7: 5: 5: 5) rows, ending with a WS row.

Shape armhole
Keeping moss st correct, cast off 4 (6: 6: 8: 9: 9) sts at beg of next row.
61 (64: 67: 68: 70: 75) sts.
Work 1 row.
Working all front slope decreases as set and all armhole shaping as set by back, cont as folls:
Dec 2 sts at armhole edge of next and 3 (3: 4: 4: 4: 5) foll alt rows, then on 2 (2: 2: 2: 2: 3) foll 4th rows **and at same time** dec 2 sts at front slope edge of 7th (next: next: 3rd: 3rd: 3rd) and 0 (1: 1: 1: 1: 2) foll 10th rows.
47 (48: 49: 50: 52: 51) sts.
Dec 2 sts at front slope edge **only** on 2nd (6th: 4th: 6th: 6th: 12th) and 3 (3: 3: 3: 2: 0) foll 10th rows, then on 0 (0: 0: 0: 1: 2) foll 12th rows.
39 (40: 41: 42: 44: 45) sts.
Work 3 (3: 3: 5: 7: 7) rows, ending with a WS row.
Inc 2 sts at armhole edge of next and foll 12th row, then on foll 10th row **and at same time** dec 2 sts at front slope edge on 7th (7th: 7th: 5th: 5th: 5th) and foll 10th (10th: 10th: 12th: 12th: 12th) row. 41 (42: 43: 44: 46: 47) sts.
Work 7 rows, ending with a WS row.

Shape shoulder
Cast off 7 (7: 7: 7: 8: 8) sts at beg of next and foll alt row, then 7 (7: 8: 8: 8: 9) sts at beg of foll alt row.
Cont in moss st on rem 20 (21: 21: 22: 22: 22) sts only for a further 7.5 (8: 8: 8.5: 8.5: 8.5) cm for back neck collar extension, ending with a WS row.
Cast off in moss st.

RIGHT FRONT
Cast on 69 (72: 75: 78: 81: 86) sts **quite loosely** using 3¾mm (US 5) needles.

Row 1 (RS): K1 (0: 1: 0: 1: 0), (P1, K1) 2 (2: 2: 3: 2: 3) times, P0 (1: 1: 0: 1: 1), wrap next st and turn.
This row sets position on moss st as given for back and left front.
Keeping moss st correct, work rows 3 to 44 as given for left front, ending with a RS row.
Cont in moss st for 25 (25: 29: 29: 29: 29) rows, ending with a WS row.
Working all front opening edge increases in same way as back side seam increases and all front side seam decreases in same way as back armhole decreases, cont as folls:
Inc 2 sts at beg of next and foll 10th row, then on 2 foll 8th rows, then on foll 6th row **and at same time** dec 2 sts at end of 5th row. 77 (80: 83: 86: 89: 94) sts.
Complete to match left front, reversing shapings.

MAKING UP
Pin the pieces out and steam gently without allowing the iron to touch the yarn.
Join both shoulder seams using back stitch or mattress stitch if preferred. Join cast-off ends of back neck collar extensions, then sew one edge to back neck. Join side seams.

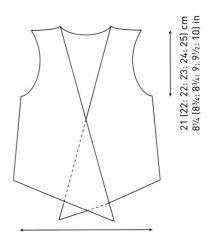

40.5 (43: 45.5: 48: 50.5: 54.5) cm
16 (17: 18: 19: 20: 21½) in

21 (22: 22: 23: 24: 25) cm
8¼ (8¾: 8¾: 9: 9½: 10) in

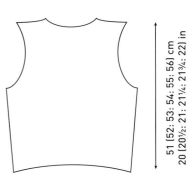

51 (52: 53: 54: 55: 56) cm
20 (20½: 21: 21¼: 21¾: 22) in

FLORENCE

TIMELESS CARDIGAN WITH MANY BUTTONS

Recommendation

Suitable for the knitter with a little experience
Please see pages 7, 8 & 9 for photographs.

	XS	S	M	L	XL	XXL	
To fit	**81**	**86**	**91**	**97**	**102**	**109**	cm
bust	32	34	36	38	40	43	in

Rowan Cashsoft 4 ply

| | 11 | 12 | 12 | 13 | 13 | 14 | x 50gm |

Photographed in Elite

Needles

1 pair 3mm (no 11) (US 2/3) needles

Buttons - 20

Tension

30 sts and 48 rows to 10 cm measured over
pattern using 3mm (US 2/3) needles.

BACK

Cast on 129 (137: 145: 153: 159: 171) sts
using 3mm (US 2/3) needles.
Row 1 (RS): K0 (0: 1: 0: 0: 0), P0 (0: 1: 1: 0:
0), K0 (0: 1: 1: 0: 1), P1 (0: 1: 1: 1: 1), *K2,
P1, K1, P1, rep from * to last 3 (2: 1: 0: 3: 4)
sts, K2 (2: 1: 0: 2: 2), P1 (0: 0: 0: 1: 1), K0 (0:
0: 0: 0: 1).
Row 2: K0 (0: 1: 0: 0: 0), P0 (0: 1: 1: 0: 0),
K0 (0: 1: 1: 0: 1), P1 (0: 1: 1: 1: 1), *P3, K1,
P1, rep from * to last 3 (2: 1: 0: 3: 4) sts, P3
(2: 1: 0: 3: 3), K0 (0: 0: 0: 0: 1).
These 2 rows form patt.
Cont in patt, shaping side seams by dec 1 st
at each end of 23rd and 8 foll 8th rows.
111 (119: 127: 135: 141: 153) sts.
Work 21 rows, ending with a WS row.
Inc 1 st at each end of next and foll 8th row,
then on 7 foll 10th rows, taking inc sts into
patt. 129 (137: 145: 153: 159: 171) sts.
Cont straight until back measures 42 (42: 43:
43: 43: 43) cm, ending with a WS row.
Shape armholes
Keeping patt correct, cast off 4 (5: 5: 6: 6: 7)
sts at beg of next 2 rows.
121 (127: 135: 141: 147: 157) sts.
Dec 1 st at each end of next 5 (5: 7: 7: 9: 11)
rows, then on foll 3 (5: 5: 7: 6: 8) alt rows,
then on 5 foll 4th rows. 95 (97: 101: 103:
107: 109) sts.
Cont straight until armhole measures 18 (19:
19: 20: 21: 22) cm, ending with a WS row.
Shape shoulders and back neck
Cast off 8 (8: 8: 8: 9: 9) sts at beg of next
2 rows. 79 (81: 85: 87: 89: 91) sts.
Next row (RS): Cast off 8 (8: 8: 8: 9: 9) sts,
patt until there are 11 (11: 13: 13: 13: 14) sts
on right needle and turn, leaving rem sts on a
holder.
Work each side of neck separately.
Cast off 4 sts at beg of next row.
Cast off rem 7 (7: 9: 9: 9: 10) sts.
With RS facing, rejoin yarn to rem sts, cast off
centre 41 (43: 43: 45: 45: 45) sts, patt to end.
Complete to match first side, reversing
shapings.

POCKET LININGS (make 2)

Cast on 32 (32: 32: 37: 37: 37) sts using
3mm (US 2/3) needles.

Row 1 (RS): K2, *P1, K1, P1, K2, rep from *
to end.
Row 2: P2, *P1, K1, P3, rep from * to end.
Rep these 2 rows 21 times more, ending with
a WS row.
Break yarn and leave sts on a holder.

LEFT FRONT

Cast on 72 (76: 80: 84: 87: 93) sts using
3mm (US 2/3) needles.
Row 1 (RS): K0 (0: 1: 0: 0: 0), P0 (0: 1: 1: 0:
0), K0 (0: 1: 1: 0: 1), P1 (0: 1: 1: 1: 1), *K2,
P1, K1, P1, rep from * to last st, K1.
Row 2: (K1, P1) twice, *P3, K1, P1, rep from *
to last 3 (2: 1: 0: 3: 4) sts, P3 (2: 1: 0: 3: 3),
K0 (0: 0: 0: 0: 1).
These 2 rows form patt.
Cont in patt, shaping side seam by dec 1 st
at beg of 23rd and 3 foll 8th rows.
68 (72: 76: 80: 83: 89) sts.
Work 5 rows, ending with a WS row.
Place pocket
Next row (RS): Patt 12 (16: 20: 14: 17: 23)
sts, slip next 32 (32: 32: 37: 37: 37) sts onto
a holder and, in their place, patt across 32 (32:
32: 37: 37: 37) sts of first pocket lining, patt
to end.
Cont in patt, shaping side seam by dec 1 st
at beg of 2nd and 4 foll 8th rows.
63 (67: 71: 75: 78: 84) sts.
Work 21 rows, ending with a WS row.
Inc 1 st at beg of next and foll 8th row, then
on 7 foll 10th rows, taking inc sts into patt.
72 (76: 80: 84: 87: 93) sts.
Cont straight until left front matches back
to beg of armhole shaping, ending with
a WS row.
Shape armhole
Keeping patt correct, cast off 4 (5: 5: 6: 6: 7)
sts at beg of next row.
68 (71: 75: 78: 81: 86) sts.
Work 1 row.
Dec 1 st at armhole edge of next 5 (5: 7: 7: 9:
11) rows, then on foll 3 (5: 5: 7: 6: 8) alt rows,
then on 5 foll 4th rows.
55 (56: 58: 59: 61: 62) sts.
Cont straight until 24 (24: 24: 28: 28: 28)
rows less have been worked than on back
to beg of shoulder shaping, ending with
a WS row.

Shape neck

Next row (RS): Patt 36 (36: 38: 39: 41: 42) sts and turn, leaving rem 19 (20: 20: 20: 20: 20) sts on a holder.

Keeping patt correct, dec 1 st at neck edge of next 8 rows, then on foll 4 alt rows, then on 1 (1: 1: 2: 2: 2) foll 4th rows. 23 (23: 25: 25: 27: 28) sts.

Work 3 rows, ending with a WS row.

Shape shoulder

Cast off 8 (8: 8: 8: 9: 9) sts at beg of next and foll alt row.

Work 1 row.

Cast off rem 7 (7: 9: 9: 9: 10) sts.

Mark positions for 10 buttons along left front opening edge – first to come in row 13, last to come level with beg of neck shaping, and rem 8 buttonholes evenly spaced between.

RIGHT FRONT

Cast on 72 (76: 80: 84: 87: 93) sts using 3mm (US 2/3) needles.

Row 1 (RS): (K1, P1) twice, *K2, P1, K1, P1, rep from * to last 3 (2: 1: 0: 3: 4) sts, K2 (2: 1: 0: 2: 2), P1 (0: 0: 0: 1: 1), K0 (0: 0: 0: 0: 1).

Row 2: K0 (0: 1: 0: 0: 0), P0 (0: 1: 1: 0: 0), K0 (0: 1: 1: 0: 1), P1 (0: 1: 1: 1: 1), *P3, K1, P1, rep from * to last st, K1.

These 2 rows form patt.

Cont in patt for a further 10 rows, ending with a WS row.

Row 13 (buttonhole row) (RS): Patt 5 sts, K2tog tbl, (yrn) twice (to make a buttonhole – work twice into this double yrn on next row), P2tog, patt to end.

Working a further 8 buttonholes in this way to correspond with positions marked for buttons on left front and noting that no further reference will be made to buttonholes, cont as folls:

Cont in patt, shaping side seam by dec 1 st at end of 12th and 3 foll 8th rows. 68 (72: 76: 80: 83: 89) sts.

Work 5 rows, ending with a WS row.

Place pocket

Next row (RS): Patt 24 (24: 24: 29: 29: 29) sts, slip next 32 (32: 32: 37: 37: 37) sts onto a holder and, in their place, patt across 32 (32: 32: 37: 37: 37) sts of second pocket lining, patt to end.

Complete to match left front, reversing shapings and working first row of neck shaping as folls:

Shape neck

Next row (RS): Patt 5 sts, K2tog tbl, (yrn) twice (to make 10th buttonhole – work twice into this double yrn on next row), P2tog, patt 10 (11: 11: 11: 11: 11) sts and slip these sts onto a holder, patt to end. 36 (36: 38: 39: 41: 42) sts.

LEFT SLEEVE
Front sleeve

Cast on 33 (34: 36: 37: 39: 40) sts using 3mm (US 2/3) needles.

Row 1 (RS): (P1, K1) twice, P1, *K2, P1, K1, P1, rep from * to last 3 (4: 1: 2: 4: 0) sts, K2 (2: 1: 2: 2: 0), P1 (1: 0: 0: 1: 0), K0 (1: 0: 0: 1: 0).

Row 2: K0 (1: 0: 0: 1: 0), P3 (3: 1: 2: 3: 0), *P1, K1, P3, rep from * to last 5 sts, (P1, K1) twice, P1.

These 2 rows form patt.

Cont in patt, shaping sleeve by inc 1 st at end of 9th (9th: 11th: 9th: 11th: 11th) and 4 (4: 0: 1: 0: 0) foll 12th rows, then on 0 (0: 3: 2: 3: 3) foll 14th rows, taking inc sts into patt. 38 (39: 40: 41: 43: 44) sts.

Work 3 (3: 7: 11: 7: 7) rows, ending with a WS row.

Break yarn and leave sts on a holder.

Back sleeve

Cast on 33 (34: 36: 37: 39: 40) sts using 3mm (US 2/3) needles.

Row 1 (RS): K0 (1: 0: 0: 1: 0), P1 (1: 0: 0: 1: 0), K2 (2: 1: 2: 2: 0), *P1, K1, P1, K2, rep from * to last 5 sts, (P1, K1) twice, P1.

Row 2: (P1, K1) twice, P1, *P3, K1, P1, rep from * to last 3 (4: 1: 2: 4: 0) sts, P3 (3: 1: 2: 3: 0), K0 (1: 0: 0: 1: 0).

These 2 rows form patt.

Cont in patt, shaping sleeve by inc 1 st at beg of 9th (9th: 11th: 9th: 11th: 11th) and 4 (4: 0: 1: 0: 0) foll 12th rows, then on 0 (0: 3: 2: 3: 3) foll 14th rows, taking inc sts into patt. 38 (39: 40: 41: 43: 44) sts.

Work 3 (3: 7: 11: 7: 7) rows, ending with a WS row.

Join sections

Next row (RS): Patt to last 7 sts of back sleeve, holding WS of sleeve front against RS of sleeve back, K tog first st of sleeve front with next st of sleeve back, (K tog next st of sleeve front with next st of sleeve back, P tog next st of sleeve front with next st of sleeve back) twice, (K tog next st of sleeve front with next st of sleeve back) twice, patt to end. 69 (71: 73: 75: 79: 81) sts.

**Now working all sts in patt as set, cont as folls:

Inc 1 st at each end of 8th (8th: 6th: 2nd: 6th: 6th) and every foll 12th (12th: 14th: 14th: 14th: 14th) row to 77 (89: 87: 97: 83: 97) sts, then on every foll 14th (14th: 16th: -: 16th: 16th) row until there are 89 (93: 93: -: 99: 103) sts, taking inc sts into patt.

Cont straight until sleeve measures 45 (46: 47: 48: 49: 50) cm, ending with a WS row.

Shape top

Keeping patt correct, cast off 4 (5: 5: 6: 6: 7) sts at beg of next 2 rows.
81 (83: 83: 85: 87: 89) sts.

Dec 1 st at each end of next 3 rows, then on foll alt row, then on foll 4th row, then on 6 foll 6th rows. 59 (61: 61: 63: 65: 67) sts.

Work 3 rows, ending with a WS row.

Dec 1 st at each end of next and every foll alt row to 51 sts, then on foll 7 rows, ending with a WS row. 37 sts.

Cast off 3 sts at beg of next 2 rows.

Cast off rem 31 sts.

RIGHT SLEEVE
Back sleeve

Work as given for front sleeve of left sleeve.

Front sleeve

Work as given for back sleeve of left sleeve.

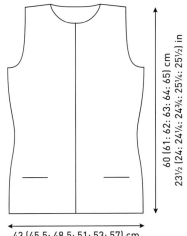

43 (45.5: 48.5: 51: 53: 57) cm
17 (18: 19: 20: 21: 22½) in

60 (61: 62: 63: 64: 65) cm
23½ (24: 24½: 24¾: 25¼: 25½) in

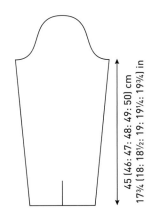

45 (46: 47: 48: 49: 50) cm
17¾ (18: 18½: 19: 19¼: 19¾) in

Continued on next page…

BETTY

LONG-LINE RANDOM STRIPE SCARF

Recommendation
Suitable for the novice knitter
Please see pages 14, 26 & 27 for photographs.

Rowan Kidsilk Haze
A	Anthracite	2	x 25gm
B	Majestic	1	x 25gm
C	Blackcurrant	1	x 25gm
D	Wicked	1	x 25gm
E	Smoke	2	x 25gm

Needles
1 pair 3¼mm (no 10) (US 3) needles

Tension
25 sts and 34 rows to 10 cm measured over
stocking stitch using 3¼mm (US 3) needles.

Finished size
Completed scarf measures 34 cm (13½ in)
wide and 265 cm (104½ in) long.

SCARF
Cast on 86 sts using 3¼mm (US 3) needles
and yarn A.
Beg with a K row, work in st st in colours
as folls:
Rows 1 to 74: Using yarn A.
Rows 75 to 84: Using yarn B.
Rows 85 to 98: Using yarn C.
Rows 99 to 110: Using yarn D.
Rows 111 to 150: Using yarn E.
Rows 151 to 158: Using yarn B.
Rows 159 to 170: Using yarn A.
Rows 171 to 182: Using yarn C.
Rows 183 to 210: Using yarn D.
Rows 211 to 248: Using yarn A.
Rows 249 to 258: Using yarn C.
Rows 259 to 266: Using yarn E.
Rows 267 to 276: Using yarn B.
Rows 277 to 288: Using yarn A.
Rows 289 to 326: Using yarn B.
Rows 327 to 342: Using yarn E.
Rows 343 to 352: Using yarn D.
Rows 353 to 362: Using yarn C.
Rows 363 to 368: Using yarn D.
Rows 369 to 406: Using yarn E.
Rows 407 to 438: Using yarn A.
Rows 439 to 446: Using yarn B.
Rows 447 to 460: Using yarn C.
Rows 461 to 470: Using yarn D.
Rows 471 to 482: Using yarn E.
Rows 483 to 494: Using yarn D.
Rows 495 to 510: Using yarn E.
Rows 511 to 530: Using yarn D.
Rows 531 to 536: Using yarn B.
Rows 537 to 556: Using yarn E.
Rows 557 to 564: Using yarn B.
Rows 565 to 572: Using yarn D.
Rows 573 to 600: Using yarn C.
Rows 601 to 652: Using yarn A.
Rows 653 to 684: Using yarn E.
Rows 685 to 694: Using yarn D.
Rows 695 to 714: Using yarn B.
Rows 715 to 724: Using yarn C.
Rows 725 to 734: Using yarn A.
Rows 735 to 746: Using yarn D.
Rows 747 to 778: Using yarn C.
Rows 779 to 788: Using yarn E.
Rows 789 to 798: Using yarn B.
Rows 799 to 808: Using yarn D.
Rows 809 to 818: Using yarn B.
Rows 819 to 832: Using yarn C.
Rows 833 to 846: Using yarn A.
Rows 847 to 854: Using yarn D.
Rows 855 to 862: Using yarn B.
Rows 863 to 900: Using yarn E.
Cast off.

Florence – Continued from previous page...

Join sections
Next row (RS): Patt to last 7 sts of front sleeve,
holding WS of sleeve front against RS of sleeve
back, K tog next st of sleeve front with first st of
sleeve back, (K tog next st of sleeve front with
next st of sleeve back, P tog next st of sleeve
front with next st of sleeve back) twice, (K tog
next st of sleeve front with next st of sleeve back)
twice, patt to end. 69 (71: 73: 75: 79: 81) sts.
Complete as given for left sleeve from **.

MAKING UP
Pin the pieces out and steam gently without
allowing the iron to touch the yarn.
Join both shoulder seams using back stitch or
mattress stitch if preferred.

Neckband
With RS facing and using 3mm (US 2/3)
needles, slip 19 (20: 20: 20: 20: 20) sts from
right front holder onto right needle, rejoin yarn
and pick up and knit 24 (24: 24: 28: 28: 28)
sts up right side of neck, 49 (51: 51: 53: 53:
53) sts from back, and 24 (24: 24: 28: 28: 28)
sts down left side of neck, then patt 19 (20:
20: 20: 20: 20) sts on left front holder.
135 (139: 139: 149: 149: 149) sts.
Next row (WS): K1, *P1, K1, rep from * to end
(remembering to work twice into double yrn
forming 10th buttonhole).
Next row: K1, *P1, K1, rep from * to end.
Rep last row 4 times more, end with a **RS** row.
Cast off in moss st (on **WS**).

Pocket tops (both alike)
Slip 32 (32: 32: 37: 37: 37) sts on pocket
holder onto 3mm (US 2/3) needles and
rejoin yarn with RS facing.
Work in patt as set for 4 rows, ending with
a WS row.
Cast off in patt.
Sew pocket linings in place on inside, then
neatly sew down ends of pocket tops.
Join side seams. Join sleeve seams.
Insert sleeves into armholes.
Sew on buttons, attaching 5 buttons to
each sleeve as in photograph to fasten
cuff opening.

CARMEN

MOSS STITCH JACKET WITH COVERED BUTTONS & CROCHET EDGING

Recommendation

Suitable for the knitter with a little experience
Please see pages 36 & 37 for photographs.

	XS	S	M	L	XL	XXL	
To fit	81	86	91	97	102	109	cm
bust	32	34	36	38	40	43	in

Rowan Felted Tweed

| | 8 | 8 | 9 | 9 | 10 | 10 | x 50gm |

Photographed in Clay

Needles

1 pair 3¾mm (no 9) (US 5) needles
3.00mm (no 11) (US C2/D3) crochet hook

Extras – 7 button frames, and pair of shoulder
pads (optional)

Tension

24 sts and 39 rows to 10 cm measured over
moss stitch using 3¾mm (US 5) needles.

CROCHET ABBREVIATIONS

ch = chain; **dc** = double crochet.

BACK

Cast on 95 (101: 107: 113: 119: 129) sts
using 3¾mm (US 5) needles.
Row 1 (RS): K0 (1: 0: 1: 0: 1), *P1, K1, rep
from * to last 1 (0: 1: 0: 1: 0) st, P1 (0: 1: 0:
1: 0).
Row 2: As row 1.
These 2 rows form moss st.
Cont in moss st until back measures 10 (10:
11: 11: 11: 11) cm, ending with a WS row.
Place markers at both ends of last row to
denote top of side seam openings.
Dec 1 st at each end of next and 3 foll 14th
rows. 87 (93: 99: 105: 111: 121) sts.
Work 17 rows, ending with a WS row.
Inc 1 st at each end of next and 2 foll 10th
rows, then on 5 foll 8th rows, taking inc sts
into moss st.
103 (109: 115: 121: 127: 137) sts.
Cont straight until back measures 44 (44: 45:
45: 45: 45) cm, ending with a WS row.
Shape armholes
Keeping moss st correct, cast off 5 (6: 6: 7: 7:
8) sts at beg of next 2 rows.
93 (97: 103: 107: 113: 121) sts.
Dec 1 st at each end of next 5 (5: 7: 7: 9: 11)
rows, then on foll 2 (3: 3: 4: 3: 4) alt rows,
then on 2 foll 4th rows.
75 (77: 79: 81: 85: 87) sts.
Cont straight until armhole measures 18 (19:
19: 20: 21: 22) cm, ending with a WS row.
Shape shoulders and back neck
Cast off 6 (6: 7: 7: 7: 8) sts at beg of next 2
rows. 63 (65: 65: 67: 71: 71) sts.
Next row (RS): Cast off 6 (6: 7: 7: 7: 8) sts,
moss st until there are 11 (11: 10: 10: 12: 11)
sts on right needle and turn, leaving rem sts
on a holder.
Work each side of neck separately.
Cast off 4 sts at beg of next row.
Cast off rem 7 (7: 6: 6: 8: 7) sts.
With RS facing, rejoin yarn to rem sts, cast off
centre 29 (31: 31: 33: 33: 33) sts, moss st to end.
Complete to match first side, reversing
shapings.

LOWER POCKET LININGS (make 2)

Cast on 23 (23: 25: 25: 27: 27) sts using
3¾mm (US 5) needles.
Row 1 (RS): P1, *K1, P1, rep from * to end.

Row 2: As row 1.
These 2 rows form moss st.
Cont in moss st for a further 27 (27: 29: 29:
29: 29) rows, ending with a **RS** row.
Break yarn and leave sts on a holder.

UPPER POCKET LININGS (make 2)

Cast on 21 (21: 23: 23: 25: 25) sts using
3¾mm (US 5) needles.
Work in moss st as given for lower pocket
linings for 27 (27: 29: 29: 29: 29) rows,
ending with a **RS** row.
Break yarn and leave sts on a holder.

LEFT FRONT

Cast on 56 (59: 62: 65: 68: 73) sts using
3¾mm (US 5) needles.
Row 1 (RS): K0 (1: 0: 1: 0: 1), *P1, K1, rep
from * to end.
Row 2: *K1, P1, rep from * to last 0 (1: 0: 1: 0:
1) st, K0 (1: 0: 1: 0: 1).
These 2 rows form moss st.
Cont in moss st until left front measures 10 (10:
11: 11: 11: 11) cm, ending with a WS row.
Place marker at end of last row to denote top
of side seam opening.
Dec 1 st at beg of next and foll 14th row.
54 (57: 60: 63: 66: 71) sts.
Work 7 rows, ending with a WS row.
Place lower pocket
Next row (RS): Moss st 12 (13: 14: 15: 16:
19) sts, cast off next 23 (23: 25: 25: 27: 27)
sts, moss st to end.
Next row: Moss st 19 (21: 21: 23: 23: 25) sts,
with **WS** facing moss st across 23 (23: 25: 25:
27: 27) sts of first lower pocket lining, moss st
to end.
Dec 1 st at beg of 5th and foll 14th row.
52 (55: 58: 61: 64: 69) sts.
Work 17 rows, ending with a WS row.
Inc 1 st at beg of next and 2 foll 10th rows,
then on 5 foll 8th rows, taking inc sts into
moss st. 60 (63: 66: 69: 72: 77) sts.
Cont straight until left front matches back to
beg of armhole shaping, ending with a WS row.
Shape armhole
Keeping moss st correct, cast off 5 (6: 6: 7: 7:
8) sts at beg of next row.
55 (57: 60: 62: 65: 69) sts.
Work 1 row.

Place upper pocket

Next row (RS): Work 2 tog, moss st 13 (13: 14: 14: 15: 17) sts, cast off next 21 (21: 23: 23: 25: 25) sts, moss st to end.

Next row: Moss st 19 (21: 21: 23: 23: 25) sts, with **WS** facing moss st across 21 (21: 23: 23: 25: 25) sts of first upper pocket lining, moss st to last 2 sts, work 2 tog.

Dec 1 st at armhole edge of next 3 (3: 5: 5: 7: 9) rows, then on foll 2 (3: 3: 4: 3: 4) alt rows, then on 2 foll 4th rows.

46 (47: 48: 49: 51: 52) sts.

Cont straight until 21 (21: 21: 25: 25: 25) rows less have been worked than on back to beg of shoulder shaping, ending with a **RS** row.

Shape neck

Cast off 16 (17: 17: 17: 17: 17) sts at beg of next row. 30 (30: 31: 32: 34: 35) sts.

Dec 1 st at neck edge of next 7 rows, then on foll 3 alt rows, then on 1 (1: 1: 2: 2: 2) foll 4th rows. 19 (19: 20: 20: 22: 23) sts.

Work 3 rows, ending with a WS row.

Shape shoulder

Cast off 6 (6: 7: 7: 7: 8) sts at beg of next and foll alt row.

Work 1 row.

Cast off rem 7 (7: 6: 6: 8: 7) sts.

Mark positions for 7 buttons along left front opening edge – first to come in row 25, last to come 2.5 cm below neck shaping, and rem 5 buttons evenly spaced between.

RIGHT FRONT

Cast on 56 (59: 62: 65: 68: 73) sts using 3¾mm (US 5) needles.

Row 1 (RS): *K1, P1, rep from * to last 0 (1: 0: 1: 0: 1) st, K0 (1: 0: 1: 0: 1).

Row 2: K0 (1: 0: 1: 0: 1), *P1, K1, rep from * to end.

These 2 rows form moss st.

Cont in moss st for a further 22 rows, ending with a WS row.

Row 25 (buttonhole row) (RS): Moss st 6 sts, cast off 3 sts (to make a buttonhole – cast on 3 sts over these cast-off sts on next row), moss st to end.

Working a further 6 buttonholes in this way to correspond with positions marked for buttons on left front and noting that no further reference will be made to buttonholes, cont as folls:

Cont in moss st until right front measures 10 (10: 11: 11: 11: 11) cm, ending with a WS row.

Place marker at beg of last row to denote top of side seam opening.

Dec 1 st at end of next and foll 14th row.

54 (57: 60: 63: 66: 71) sts.

Work 7 rows, ending with a WS row.

Place lower pocket

Next row (RS): Moss st 19 (21: 21: 23: 23: 25) sts, cast off next 23 (23: 25: 25: 27: 27) sts, moss st to end.

Next row: Moss st 12 (13: 14: 15: 16: 19) sts, with **WS** facing moss st across 23 (23: 25: 25: 27: 27) sts of 2nd lower pocket lining, moss st to end.

Dec 1 st at end of 5th and foll 14th row.

52 (55: 58: 61: 64: 69) sts.

Work 17 rows, ending with a WS row.

Inc 1 st at end of next and 2 foll 10th rows, then on 5 foll 8th rows, taking inc sts into moss st. 60 (63: 66: 69: 72: 77) sts.

Cont straight until right front matches back to beg of armhole shaping, ending with a **RS** row.

Shape armhole

Keeping moss st correct, cast off 5 (6: 6: 7: 7: 8) sts at beg of next row.

55 (57: 60: 62: 65: 69) sts.

Place upper pocket

Next row (RS): Moss st 19 (21: 21: 23: 23: 25) sts, cast off next 21 (21: 23: 23: 25: 25) sts, moss st to last 2 sts, work 2 tog.

Next row: Work 2 tog, moss st 12 (12: 13: 13: 14: 16) sts, with **WS** facing moss st across 21 (21: 23: 23: 25: 25) sts of 2nd upper pocket lining, moss st to end.

Complete to match left front, reversing shapings.

SLEEVES (both alike)

First section

Cast on 23 (24: 25: 26: 28: 29) sts using 3¾mm (US 5) needles.

Row 1 (RS): *P1, K1, rep from * to last 1 (0: 1: 0: 0: 1) st, P1 (0: 1: 0: 0: 1).

Row 2: P1 (0: 1: 0: 0: 1), *K1, P1, rep from * to end.

These 2 rows form moss st.

Cont in moss st, shaping sleeve by inc 1 st at end of 9th (9th: 9th: 9th: 11th: 9th) and 1 (1: 1: 1: 0: 1) foll 12th row, taking inc sts into patt. 25 (26: 27: 28: 29: 31) sts.

Work 1 (1: 1: 1: 11: 1) rows, ending with a WS row.

Break yarn and leave sts on a holder.

Second section

Cast on 23 (24: 25: 26: 28: 29) sts using 3¾mm (US 5) needles.

Row 1 (RS): P1 (0: 1: 0: 0: 1), *K1, P1, rep from * to end.

Row 2: *P1, K1, rep from * to last 1 (0: 1: 0: 0: 1) st, P1 (0: 1: 0: 0: 1).

These 2 rows form moss st.

Cont in moss st, shaping sleeve by inc 1 st at beg of 9th (9th: 9th: 9th: 11th: 9th) and 1 (1: 1: 1: 0: 1) foll 12th row, taking inc sts into patt.

25 (26: 27: 28: 29: 31) sts.

Work 1 (1: 1: 1: 11: 1) rows, ending with a WS row.

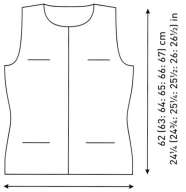

43 (45.5: 48: 50.5: 53: 57) cm
17 (18: 19: 20: 21: 22½) in

62 (63: 64: 65: 66: 67) cm
24¼ (24¾: 25¼: 25½: 26: 26½) in

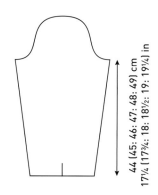

44 (45: 46: 47: 48: 49) cm
17¼ (17¾: 18: 18½: 19: 19¼) in

Join sections

Next row (RS): Moss st to last st of second section, inc in last st, then moss st across sts of first section. 51 (53: 55: 57: 59: 63) sts.
Cont in moss st across all sts, inc 1 st at each end of 10th (10th: 10th: 10th: 2nd: 10th) and every foll 12th (12th: 12th: 12th: 14th: 12th) row to 63 (75: 59: 71: 81: 69) sts, then on every foll 14th (-: 14th: 14th: -: 14th) row until there are 71 (-: 75: 79: -: 85) sts, taking inc sts into moss st.
Cont straight until sleeve measures 44 (45: 46: 47: 48: 49) cm, ending with a WS row.

Shape top
Keeping moss st correct, cast off 5 (6: 6: 7: 7: 8) sts at beg of next 2 rows.
61 (63: 63: 65: 67: 69) sts.
Dec 1 st at each end of next 3 rows, then on foll alt row, then on foll 4th row, then on 4 foll 6th rows, then on foll 4th row. 41 (43: 43: 45: 47: 49) sts.
Work 3 rows, ending with a WS row.
Dec 1 st at each end of next and every foll alt row to 35 sts, then on foll 5 rows, ending with a WS row.
Cast off rem 25 sts.

MAKING UP
Pin the pieces out and steam gently without allowing the iron to touch the yarn.
Join both shoulder seams using back stitch or mattress stitch if preferred.
Join side seams, leaving seams open below markers.
Join sleeve seams. Insert sleeves into armholes.

Back hem edging
With RS facing and using 3.00mm (US C2/ D3) crochet hook, attach yarn at marker at top of left side seam opening, 1 ch (does NOT count as st), work in dc evenly down left side seam opening, across back cast-on edge, then up right side seam opening to marker, working 3 dc into each corner point, do **NOT** turn.
Now work 1 row of crab st (dc worked from left to right, instead of right to left) around back hem and opening edges.
Fasten off.

Front hem, opening and neck edging
Work as given for back hem edging, beg at marker at top of right side seam opening, working down right side seam opening, across right front cast-on edge, up right front opening edge, around neck, down left front opening edge, across left front cast-on edge, then up left side seam opening to marker.

Cuff edging
Work as given for back hem edging, beg and ending at top of cuff opening.

Pocket tops (all 4 alike)
Work as given for back hem edging, working across pocket cast-off edge.
Sew pocket linings in place on inside, then neatly sew down ends of pocket tops.
Following instructions on packet, cover button frames with yarn, then sew on buttons.

Recommendation
Suitable for the knitter with a little experience
Please see pages 18, 20 & 22 for photographs.

	XS	S	M	L	XL	XXL	
To fit	**81**	**86**	**91**	**97**	**102**	**109**	**cm**
bust	32	34	36	38	40	43	in

Rowan Kid Classic
9 10 10 11 11 12 x 50gm
Photographed in Peat

Needles
1 pair 3¾mm (no 9) (US 5) needles
1 pair 4mm (no 8) (US 6) needles
1 pair 4½mm (no 7) (US 7) needles

Tension
21 sts and 27 rows to 10 cm measured over
stocking stitch using 4½mm (US 7) needles.

Special abbreviations
MP = make picot as folls: cast on 1 st, cast off
1 st – one st on right needle.

BESSIE
BELTED CARDIGAN WITH SIDE POCKETS

BACK
Cast on 91 (95: 101: 107: 111: 119) sts
using 4½mm (US 7) needles.
Row 1 (RS): K1 (1: 0: 1: 1: 1), *P1, K1,
rep from * to last 0 (0: 1: 0: 0: 0) st,
P0 (0: 1: 0: 0: 0).
Row 2: P1 (1: 0: 1: 1: 1), *K1, P1, rep from *
to last 0 (0: 1: 0: 0: 0) st, K0 (0: 1: 0: 0: 0).
These 2 rows form rib.
Work in rib for a further 18 rows, ending with
a WS row.
Beg with a K row, work in st st as folls:
Work 6 rows, ending with a WS row.
Next row (dec) (RS): K3, K2tog, K to last 5 sts,
K2tog tbl, K3.
Working all side seam decreases as set by last
row, dec 1 st at each end of 12th and foll 12th
row, then on 2 foll 10th rows.
81 (85: 91: 97: 101: 109) sts.
Work 17 rows, ending with a WS row.
Next row (inc) (RS): K3, M1, K to last 3 sts,
M1, K3.
Working all side seam increases as set by
last row, inc 1 st at each end of 8th and
foll 8th row, then on 2 foll 6th rows.
91 (95: 101: 107: 111: 119) sts.
Work 5 (5: 7: 7: 7: 7) rows, ending with
a WS row.
(Back should measure 45 (45: 46: 46:
46: 46) cm.)
Shape raglan armholes
Cast off 8 sts at beg of next 2 rows.
75 (79: 85: 91: 95: 103) sts.
Work 2 (2: 0: 0: 0: 0) rows.
Next row (dec) (RS): K1, K2tog, K to last 3 sts,
K2tog tbl, K1.
Working all raglan armhole decreases as set
by last row, dec 1 st at each end of 6th (4th:
2nd: 2nd: 2nd: 2nd) and foll 0 (0: 3: 6: 9: 16)
alt rows, then on 10 (11: 11: 10: 9: 6) foll 4th
rows.
51 (53: 53: 55: 55: 55) sts.
Work 3 rows, ending with a WS row.
Cast off.

LEFT POCKET LINING
Cast on 30 (30: 32: 32: 34: 34) sts using
4½mm (US 7) needles.
Beg with a K row, work in st st as folls:
Work 6 rows, ending with a WS row.

Row 7 (RS): K3, K2tog, K to end.
Working side seam dec as set by last row, work
a further 21 rows, dec 1 st at beg of 12th of
these rows and ending with a WS row.
28 (28: 30: 30: 32: 32) sts.
Break yarn and leave sts on a holder.

LEFT FRONT
Cast on 60 (62: 65: 68: 70: 74) sts using
4½mm (US 7) needles.
Row 1 (RS): K1 (1: 0: 1: 1: 1), *P1, K1, rep
from * to last 15 sts, P1, K14.
Row 2: MP, K until there are 14 sts on right
needle, *K1, P1, rep from * to last 0 (0: 1: 0: 0:
0) st, K0 (0: 1: 0: 0: 0).
Row 3: As row 1.
Row 4: K14, *K1, P1, rep from * to last 0 (0: 1:
0: 0: 0) st, K0 (0: 1: 0: 0: 0).
These 4 rows set the sts – front opening edge
14 sts worked in g st with picot on every 4th
row and all other sts in rib.
Cont as set for a further 16 rows, ending with
a WS row.
Next row (RS): Knit.
Next row: Patt 14 sts, P to end.
These 2 rows set the sts for rest of left front –
front opening edge 14 sts in patt as set with all
other sts now in st st.
Work 4 rows, ending with a WS row.
Working all side seam decreases as set by
back, dec 1 st at beg of next and foll 12th row.
58 (60: 63: 66: 68: 72) sts.
Work 9 rows, ending with a WS row.
Place pocket
Next row (RS): Holding RS of left pocket lining
against WS of left front, K tog first st of each
section, K tog 2nd st of each section, slip next
26 (26: 28: 28: 30: 30) sts of left front onto
a holder and, in their place, K across rem
26 (26: 28: 28: 30: 30) sts of left pocket
lining, patt to end.
Cont as set, dec 1 st at beg of 2nd and 2 foll
10th rows. 55 (57: 60: 63: 65: 69) sts.
Work 17 rows, ending with a WS row.
Working all side seam increases as set by
back, inc 1 st at beg of next and 2 foll 8th
rows, then on 2 foll 6th rows.
60 (62: 65: 68: 70: 74) sts.
Work 5 (5: 7: 7: 7: 7) rows, ending with
a WS row.

Shape raglan armhole

Cast off 8 sts at beg of next row.
52 (54: 57: 60: 62: 66) sts.
Work 3 (3: 1: 1: 1: 1) rows.
Working all raglan armhole decreases as set by back, dec 1 st at beg of next and 1 (0: 0: 0: 0: 0) foll 6th row, then on foll 0 (0: 4: 7: 10: 17) alt rows, then on 10 (12: 11: 10: 9: 6) foll 4th rows. 40 (41: 41: 42: 42: 42) sts.
Work 3 rows, ending with a WS row.
Break yarn and leave sts on a holder.

RIGHT POCKET LINING

Cast on 30 (30: 32: 32: 34: 34) sts using 4½mm (US 7) needles.
Beg with a K row, work in st st as folls:
Work 6 rows, ending with a WS row.
Row 7 (RS): K to last 5 sts, K2tog tbl, K3.
Working side seam dec as set by last row, work a further 21 rows, dec 1 st at end of 12th of these rows and ending with a WS row.
28 (28: 30: 30: 32: 32) sts.
Break yarn and leave sts on a holder.

RIGHT FRONT

Cast on 60 (62: 65: 68: 70: 74) sts using 4½mm (US 7) needles.
Row 1 (RS): MP, K until there are 14 sts on right needle, *P1, K1, rep from * to last 0 (0: 1: 0: 0: 0) st, P0 (0: 1: 0: 0: 0).
Row 2: P1 (1: 0: 1: 1: 1), *K1, P1, rep from * to last 15 sts, K15.
Row 3: K14, *P1, K1, rep from * to last 0 (0: 1: 0: 0: 0) st, P0 (0: 1: 0: 0: 0).
Row 4: As row 2.
These 4 rows set the sts – front opening edge 14 sts worked in g st with picot on every 4th row and all other sts in rib.
Cont as set for a further 16 rows, ending with a WS row.
Next row (RS): Patt 14 sts, K to end.
Next row: P to last 14 sts, K14.
These 2 rows set the sts for rest of right front – front opening edge 14 sts in patt as set with all other sts now in st st.
Work 4 rows, ending with a WS row.
Working all side seam decreases as set by back, dec 1 st at end of next and foll 12th row.
58 (60: 63: 66: 68: 72) sts.
Work 9 rows, ending with a WS row.
Place pocket
Next row (RS): Patt to last 28 (28: 30: 30: 32: 32) sts, slip next 26 (26: 28: 28: 30: 30) sts of right front onto a holder and, in their place, K across first 26 (26: 28: 28: 30: 30) sts of right pocket lining, holding RS of right pocket lining against WS of right front, K tog next st of each

section, K tog last st of each section.
Complete to match left front, reversing shapings. Do NOT break off yarn but set aside this ball of yarn – it will be used for collar.

SLEEVES

Cast on 39 (41: 43: 45: 47: 49) sts using 4½mm (US 7) needles.
Beg with a K row and working all increases in same way as side seam increases, work in st st, shaping sides by inc 1 st at each end of 7th and 6 (5: 4: 2: 1: 0) foll 8th rows, then on every foll 10th row until there are 63 (65: 67: 69: 71: 73) sts.
Cont straight until sleeve measures 44 (45: 46: 47: 48: 49) cm, ending with a WS row.
Shape raglan
Cast off 8 sts at beg of next 2 rows.
47 (49: 51: 53: 55: 57) sts.
Work 2 rows.
Working all raglan decreases in same way as back and front raglan armhole decreases, dec 1 st at each end of next and 10 foll 4th rows, then on every foll alt row until 17 sts rem.
Work 1 row, ending with a WS row.
Cast off.

MAKING UP

Pin the pieces out and steam gently without allowing the iron to touch the yarn.
Join all raglan seams using back stitch or mattress stitch if preferred.
Collar
With RS facing, using 4½mm (US 7) needles and ball of yarn set aside with right front, work across 40 (41: 41: 42: 42: 42) sts on right front holder as folls: patt to last 2 sts, K2tog, pick up and knit 15 sts from top of right sleeve, 49 (51: 51: 53: 53: 53) sts from back, and 15 sts from top of left sleeve, work across 40 (41: 41: 42: 42: 42) sts on left front holder as folls: K2tog tbl, patt to end. 157 (161: 161: 165: 165: 165) sts.
Next row (WS): Patt until there are 14 sts on right needle, P1, *K1, P1, rep from * to last 14 sts, K14.
Next row: Patt until there are 14 sts on right needle, K1, *P1, K1, rep from * to last 14 sts, K14.
These 2 rows set the sts.
Cont as set until collar measures 15 cm from pick-up row, ending with a WS row.
Cast off in patt.
Pocket tops (both alike)
Slip 26 (26: 28: 28: 30: 30) sts on pocket holder onto 4mm (US 6) needles and rejoin yarn with RS facing.

Beg with a K row, work in st st for 4 rows, ending with a WS row.
Cast off.
Join side and sleeve seams. Sew pocket linings in place on inside, then neatly sew down ends of pocket tops.
Belt
Using 3¾mm (US 5) needles work picot cast-on as folls: cast on 4 sts, cast off 1 st, slip st on right needle back onto left needle, (cast on 3 sts, cast off 1 st, slip st on right needle back onto left needle) 5 times, cast on 1 st. 14 sts.
Row 1 (RS): MP, K to last 2 sts, inc in next st, K1. 15 sts.
Row 2: MP, K to last 2 sts, K2tog tbl. 14 sts.
Rep last 2 rows until belt measures 135 (140: 145: 150: 155: 160) cm, ending with a WS row. 14 sts.
Now work picot cast-off as folls: cast off 2 sts, *slip st on right needle back onto left needle, cast on 2 sts, cast off 4 sts, rep from * to end.
Make two 15 cm long tassels and attach one to each end of belt.

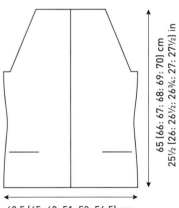

43.5 (45: 48: 51: 53: 56.5) cm
17 (18: 19: 20: 21: 22¼) in

65 (66: 67: 68: 69: 70) cm
25½ (26: 26½: 26¾: 27: 27½) in

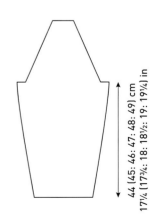

44 (45: 46: 47: 48: 49) cm
17¼ (17¾: 18: 18½: 19: 19¾) in

Recommendation

Suitable for the knitter with a little experience
Please see pages 19, 21 & 22 for photographs.

	S	M	L	XL	
To fit	97	102	107	112	cm
chest	38	40	42	44	in

Rowan Baby Alpaca DK

| | 12 | 13 | 13 | 14 | x 50gm |

Photographed in Cheviot

Needles

1 pair 2¾mm (no 12) (US 2) needles
1 pair 3¼mm (no 10) (US 3) needles

Buttons - 6

Tension

24 sts and 32 rows to 10 cm measured over
stocking stitch using 3¼mm (US 3) needles.

RALPH
CLOSE FITTING BUTTON THROUGH SWEATER

BACK

Cast on 122 (130: 134: 142) sts using
2¾mm (US 2) needles.
Row 1 (RS): P2, *K2, P2, rep from * to end.
Row 2: K2, *P2, K2, rep from * to end.
These 2 rows form rib.
Cont in rib for a further 20 rows, inc (dec: inc:
dec) 1 st at centre of last row and ending with
a WS row.
123 (129: 135: 141) sts.
Change to 3¼mm (US 3) needles.
Beg with a K row, work in st st until back
measures 48cm, ending with a WS row.
Shape armholes
Cast off 5 (6: 7: 8) sts at beg of next 2 rows.
113 (117: 121: 125) sts.
Dec 1 st at each end of next 3 rows, then
on foll 5 alt rows, then on 3 foll 4th rows.
91 (95: 99: 103) sts.
Cont straight until armhole measures 20 (21:
22: 23) cm, ending with a WS row.
Shape shoulders and back neck
Cast off 8 (8: 9: 9) sts at beg of next 2 rows.
75 (79: 81: 85) sts.
Next row (RS): Cast off 8 (8: 9: 9) sts,
K until there are 12 (13: 13: 14) sts on
right needle and turn, leaving rem sts
on a holder.
Work each side of neck separately.
Cast off 4 sts at beg of next row.
Cast off rem 8 (9: 9: 10) sts.
With RS facing, rejoin yarn to rem sts, cast off
centre 35 (37: 37: 39) sts, K to end.
Complete to match first side, reversing
shapings.

FRONT

Work as given for back until 116 (118: 118:
120) rows less have been worked than on
back to beg of shoulder shaping, ending with
a WS row.
Divide for front opening
Next row (RS): K64 (67: 70: 73) and turn,
leaving rem sts on a holder.
Work each side of neck separately.
Next row (WS): K5, P to end.
Next row: Knit.
These 2 rows set the sts – front opening edge
5 sts in g st with all other sts still in st st.
Work 9 rows, ending with a WS row.

Next row (buttonhole row) (RS): K to last
5 sts, K2tog tbl, (yfwd) twice (to make a
buttonhole – work twice into double yfwd
on next row), K2tog, K1.
Making a further 4 buttonholes in this way
on every foll 16th row and noting that no
further reference will be made to buttonholes,
cont as folls:
Cont as set until front matches back to beg
of armhole shaping, ending with a WS row.
Shape armhole
Cast off 5 (6: 7: 8) sts at beg of next row.
59 (61: 63: 65) sts.
Work 1 row.
Dec 1 st at armhole edge of next 3 rows, then
on foll 5 alt rows, then on 3 foll 4th rows.
48 (50: 52: 54) sts.
Cont straight until 24 (26: 26: 28) rows less
have been worked than on back to beg of
shoulder shaping, ending with a WS row.
Shape front neck
Next row (RS): K35 (37: 39: 41) and turn,
leaving rem 13 sts on a holder.
Dec 1 st at neck edge of next 6 rows, then on
foll 3 (4: 4: 5) alt rows, then on 2 foll 4th rows.
24 (25: 27: 28) sts.
Work 3 rows, ending with a WS row.
Shape shoulder
Cast off 8 (8: 9: 9) sts at beg of next and foll
alt row.
Work 1 row.
Cast off rem 8 (9: 9: 10) sts.
With RS facing, rejoin yarn to rem sts, cast
on 5 sts, K to end. 64 (67: 70: 73) sts.
Next row (WS): P to last 5 sts, K5.
Next row: Knit.
These 2 rows set the sts – front opening edge
5 sts in g st with all other sts still in st st.
Complete to match first side, reversing
shapings and working first row of neck shaping
as folls:
Shape front neck
Next row (RS): K13 and slip these sts onto
a holder, K to end. 35 (37: 39: 41) sts.

SLEEVES (both alike)

Cast on 64 (66: 68: 70) sts using 2¾mm (US
2) needles.
Row 1 (RS): K1 (2: 1: 2), P2, *K2, P2, rep from
* to 1 (2: 1: 2) sts, K1 (2: 1: 2).

Row 2: P1 (2: 1: 2), K2, *P2, K2, rep from * to 1 (2: 1: 2) sts, P1 (2: 1: 2).
These 2 rows form rib.
Cont in rib, inc 1 st at each end of 13th (11th: 11th: 9th) and foll 0 (0: 0: 12th) row, taking inc sts into rib. 66 (68: 70: 74) sts.
Work 11 (13: 13: 3) rows, ending with a WS row.
Change to 3¼mm (US 3) needles.
Beg with a K row, now work in st st as folls:
Work 4 (0: 0: 8) rows, ending with a WS row.
Next row (inc) (RS): K3, M1, K to last 3 sts, M1, K3.
Working all increases as set by last row, inc 1 st at each end of 16th (14th: 14th: 12th) and every foll 16th (14th: 14th: 12th) row to 78 (76: 90: 82) sts, then on every foll 18th (16th: -: 14th) row until there are 82 (86: -: 94) sts.
Cont straight until sleeve measures 51 (52: 53: 54) cm, ending with a WS row.

Shape top
Cast off 5 (6: 7: 8) sts at beg of next 2 rows.
72 (74: 76: 78) sts.
Dec 1 st at each end of next 3 rows, then on foll alt row, then on 7 foll 4th rows.
50 (52: 54: 56) sts.
Work 1 row.
Dec 1 st at each end of next and every foll alt row to 42 sts, then on foll 5 rows, ending with a WS row. Cast off rem 32 sts.

MAKING UP
Pin the pieces out and steam gently without allowing the iron to touch the yarn.
Join both shoulder seams using back stitch or mattress stitch if preferred.

Neckband
With RS facing and using 2¾mm (US 2) needles, slip 13 sts on right front holder onto right needle, rejoin yarn and pick up and knit 26 (28: 28: 30) sts up right side of neck, 42 (46: 46: 50) sts from back, and 26 (28: 28: 30) sts down left side of neck, then patt across 13 sts on left front holder, making 6th buttonhole in this row. 120 (128: 128: 136) sts.
Row 1 (WS): K7, *P2, K2, rep from * to last 5 sts, K5.
Row 2: K5, *P2, K2, rep from * to last 7 sts, P2, K5.
Rep last 2 rows twice more, ending with a **RS** row.
Cast off in patt (on **WS**).
Join side seams. Join sleeve seams. Insert sleeves into armholes. Neatly sew cast-on edge at base of front opening in place on inside, then sew on buttons.

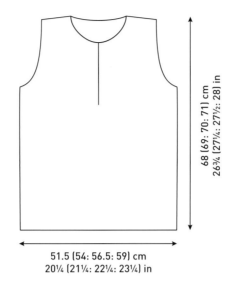

51.5 (54: 56.5: 59) cm
20¼ (21¼: 22¼: 23¼) in

68 (69: 70: 71) cm
26¾ (27¼: 27½: 28) in

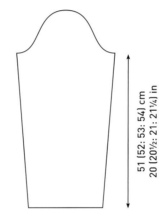

51 (52: 53: 54) cm
20 (20½: 21: 21¼) in

ISADORA

RAGLAN TUNIC WITH SHAPED LOWER FRONT EDGE & POCKETS

Recommendation

Suitable for the knitter with a little experience
Please see pages 24 & 25 for photographs.

	XS	S	M	L	XL	XXL	
To fit	**81**	**86**	**91**	**97**	**102**	**109**	cm
bust	32	34	36	38	40	43	in

Rowan Kid Classic

| 9 | 10 | 10 | 11 | 11 | 12 | x 50gm |

Photographed in Peat

Needles

1 pair 4mm (no 8) (US 6) needles
1 pair 4½mm (no 7) (US 7) needles
4mm (no 8) (US 6) circular needle
3¾mm (no 9) (US 5) circular needle

Tension

21 sts and 27 rows to 10 cm measured over
stocking stitch using 4½mm (US 7) needles.

BACK

Cast on 111 (117: 123: 127: 133: 141) sts
using 4½mm (US 7) needles.
Row 1 (RS): K2 (0: 0: 0: 0: 2), P2 (2: 0: 2: 0:
2), *K3, P2, rep from * to last 2 (0: 3: 0: 3: 2)
sts, K2 (0: 3: 0: 3: 2).
Row 2: P2 (0: 0: 0: 0: 2), K2 (2: 0: 2: 0: 2),
*P3, K2, rep from * to last 2 (0: 3: 0: 3: 2) sts,
P2 (0: 3: 0: 3: 2).
These 2 rows form rib.
Work in rib for a further 16 rows, ending with
a WS row.
Beg with a K row, work in st st as folls:
Work 22 rows, ending with a WS row.
Next row (dec) (RS): K3, K2tog, K to last 5 sts,
K2tog tbl, K3.
Working all side seam decreases as set by last
row, dec 1 st at each end of 18th and 4 foll
18th rows. 99 (105: 111: 115: 121: 129) sts.
Cont straight until back measures 56 (56: 57:
57: 57: 57) cm, ending with a WS row.
Shape raglan armholes
Cast off 5 sts at beg of next 2 rows.
89 (95: 101: 105: 111: 119) sts.
Work 2 (2: 2: 2: 2: 0) rows.
Next row (RS): K1, K2tog, K to last 3 sts,
K2tog tbl, K1.
Working all raglan armhole decreases as set
by last row, dec 1 st at each end of 4th (4th:
4th: 4th: 4th: 2nd) and 6 (5: 2: 2: 1: 0) foll
4th rows, then on foll 9 (12: 18: 19: 23: 28)
alt rows. 55 (57: 57: 59: 59: 59) sts.
Work 1 row, ending with a WS row.
Cast off.

FRONT

Cast on 119 (125: 131: 135: 141: 149) sts
using 4½mm (US 7) needles.
Row 1 (RS): K1 (0: 2: 0: 2: 1), P2 (1: 2: 1: 2:
2), *K3, P2, rep from * to last 1 (4: 2: 4: 2: 1)
sts, K1 (3: 1: 3: 2: 1), P0 (1: 0: 1: 0: 0).
Row 2: P1 (0: 2: 0: 2: 1), K2 (1: 2: 1: 2: 2),
*P3, K2, rep from * to last 1 (4: 2: 4: 2: 1) sts,
P1 (3: 1: 3: 2: 1), K0 (1: 0: 1: 0: 0).
These 2 rows form rib.
Cont in rib, dec 1 st at each end of 5th and foll
6th row. 115 (121: 127: 131: 137: 145) sts.
Work a further 5 rows, ending with a WS row.
Beg with a K row, work in st st and shape
lower left hem edge as folls:

Row 1 (RS): K2tog, K4, wrap next st (by
slipping next st on left needle onto right
needle, taking yarn to opposite side of work
between needles and then slipping same st
back onto left needle – when working back
across wrapped sts, work the wrapped st and
the wrapping loop tog as one st) and turn.
Row 2: Purl.
Row 3: K8, wrap next st and turn.
Row 4: Purl.
Row 5: K11, wrap next st and turn.
Row 6: Purl.
Row 7: K3, K2tog, K9, wrap next st and turn.
Row 8: Purl.
Row 9: K16, wrap next st and turn.
Row 10: Purl.
Row 11: K20, wrap next st and turn.
Row 12: Purl.
Row 13: K25, wrap next st and turn.
Row 14: Purl.
Row 15: K31, wrap next st and turn.
Row 16: Purl.
Row 17: K38, wrap next st and turn.
Row 18: Purl.
Row 19: K46, wrap next st and turn.
Row 20: Purl.
This completes lower left hem edge shaping.
Next row (RS): K to last 2 sts, K2tog.
Now shape lower right hem edge as folls:
Row 1 (WS): P5, wrap next st and turn.
Row 2: Knit.
Row 3: P8, wrap next st and turn.
Row 4: Knit.
Row 5: P11, wrap next st and turn.
Row 6: K6, K2tog tbl, K3.
Row 7: P13, wrap next st and turn.
Row 8: Knit.
Row 9: P16, wrap next st and turn.
Row 10: Knit.
Row 11: P20, wrap next st and turn.
Row 12: Knit.
Row 13: P25, wrap next st and turn.
Row 14: Knit.
Row 15: P31, wrap next st and turn.
Row 16: Knit.
Row 17: P38, wrap next st and turn.
Row 18: Knit.
Row 19: P46, wrap next st and turn.
Row 20: Knit.
This completes lower right hem edge shaping.

Next row (WS): P to end.

111 (117: 123: 127: 133: 141) sts.
Working all side seam decreases as set by back, dec 1 st at each end of next and foll 18th row. 107 (113: 119: 123: 129: 137) sts.
Work 1 row, ending with a WS row.

Shape pocket

Next row (RS): K19 (22: 24: 26: 28: 32) and slip these sts onto a holder for left side front, K69 (69: 71: 71: 73: 73) and turn, leaving rem 19 (22: 24: 26: 28: 32) sts on a second holder for right side front.
Work on centre 69 (69: 71: 71: 73: 73) sts only for pocket front as folls:

Next row (WS): K6, P to last 6 sts, K6.

Next row: Knit.

Last 2 rows set the sts – pocket opening edge sts in g st with all other sts still in st st.
Cont as set for a further 35 rows, ending with a WS row.
Break yarn and leave these sts on a spare needle.

Shape pocket back

Slip 19 (22: 24: 26: 28: 32) sts on left side front holder onto right needle and rejoin yarn, turn and cast on 69 (69: 71: 71: 73: 73) sts (for pocket back), turn and K across 19 (22: 24: 26: 28: 32) sts on right side front holder. 107 (113: 119: 123: 129: 137) sts.
Cont in st st across all sts, dec 1 st at each end of 16th and foll 18th row.
103 (109: 115: 119: 125: 133) sts.
Work 3 rows, ending with a WS row.

Join sections

Next row (RS): K first 17 (20: 22: 24: 26: 30) sts, holding WS of pocket front against RS of pocket back, K tog first st of pocket front with next st of pocket back, (K tog next st of pocket front with next st of pocket back) 68 (68: 70: 70: 72: 72) times, K rem 17 (20: 22: 24: 26: 30) sts. 103 (109: 115: 119: 125: 133) sts.
Dec 1 st at each end of 14th and foll 18th row. 99 (105: 111: 115: 121: 129) sts.
Cont straight until side seam edges of front match back to beg of raglan armhole shaping, ending with a WS row. (**Note:** centre front section is 20 rows shorter than back.)

Shape raglan armholes

Cast off 5 sts at beg of next 2 rows.
89 (95: 101: 105: 111: 119) sts.
Work 2 (2: 2: 2: 2: 0) rows.
Working all raglan armhole decreases as set by back, dec 1 st at each end of next and 7 (6: 3: 3: 2: 0) foll 4th rows, then on foll 3 (6: 12: 12: 16: 22) alt rows.
67 (69: 69: 73: 73: 73) sts.
Work 1 row, ending with a WS row.

Shape neck

Next row (RS): K3, K2tog, K7 (7: 7: 9: 9: 9) and turn, leaving rem sts on a holder.
Work each side of neck separately.
Dec 1 st at neck edge of next 5 rows **and at same time** dec 1 st at raglan armhole edge of 2nd and foll alt row. 4 (4: 4: 6: 6: 6) sts.

Sizes L, XL and XXL only

Next row (RS): K3, K3tog. 4 sts.
Work 1 row.

All sizes

Next row (RS): K1, K3tog.

Next row: P2.

Next row: K2tog and fasten off.
With RS facing, rejoin yarn to rem sts, cast off centre 43 (45: 45: 45: 45: 45) sts, K to last 5 sts, K2tog tbl, K3.
Dec 1 st at neck edge of next 5 rows **and at same time** dec 1 st at raglan armhole edge of 2nd and foll alt row. 4 (4: 4: 6: 6: 6) sts.

Sizes L, XL and XXL only

Next row (RS): K3tog tbl, K3. 4 sts.
Work 1 row.

All sizes

Next row (RS): K3tog tbl, K1.

Next row: P2.

Next row: K2tog and fasten off.

SLEEVES (both alike)

Cast on 43 (45: 47: 49: 51: 53) sts using 4mm (US 6) needles.
Beg with a K row, work in st st for 8 rows, ending with a WS row.
Change to 4½mm (US 7) needles.
Cont in st st, shaping sides by inc 1 st at each end of next and every foll 8th row to 67 (67: 57: 55: 65: 65) sts, then on every foll 10th row until there are 69 (71: 71: 73: 77: 79) sts.
Cont straight until sleeve measures 44 (45: 46: 47: 48: 49) cm, ending with a WS row.

Shape raglan

Cast off 5 sts at beg of next 2 rows.
59 (61: 61: 63: 67: 69) sts.
Working all raglan decreases in same way as back raglan armhole decreases, dec 1 st at each end of 3rd and 10 foll 4th rows, then on every foll alt row until 35 sts rem.
Work 1 row, ending with a WS row.

Left sleeve only

Dec 1 st at each end of next row, then cast off 10 sts at beg of foll row. 23 sts.
Dec 1 st at beg of next row, then cast off 11 sts at beg of foll row.

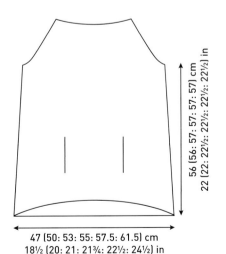

56 (56: 57: 57: 57: 57) cm
22 (22: 22½: 22½: 22½: 22½) in

47 (50: 53: 55: 57.5: 61.5) cm
18½ (20: 21: 21¾: 22½: 24½) in

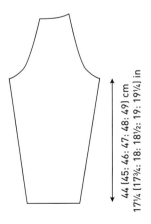

44 (45: 46: 47: 48: 49) cm
17¼ (17¾: 18: 18½: 19: 19¼) in

Right sleeve only
Cast off 11 sts at beg and dec 1 st at end
of next row. 23 sts.
Work 1 row.
Rep last 2 rows once more.
Both sleeves
Cast off rem 11 sts.

MAKING UP
Pin the pieces out and steam gently without
allowing the iron to touch the yarn.
Join all raglan armhole seams using back
stitch or mattress stitch if preferred.
Neckband
With RS facing and using 4mm (US 6) circular
needle, beg and ending at left back raglan
seam, pick up and knit 31 sts from top of left
sleeve, 9 (9: 9: 11: 11: 11) sts down left side
of front neck, 43 (43: 43: 44: 44: 44) sts from
front, 9 (9: 9: 11: 11: 11) sts up right side of
front neck, 31 sts from top of right sleeve, then
52 (57: 57: 57: 57: 57) sts from back. 175
(180: 180: 185: 185: 185) sts.
Round 1 (RS): *K3, P2, rep from * to end.
Rounds 2 to 10: As round 1.
Round 11: (K3, P2tog) 6 times, (K3, P2) 12
(12: 12: 13: 13: 13) times, (K3, P2tog) 6
times, (K3, P2) 11 (12: 12: 12: 12: 12) times.
163 (168: 168: 173: 173: 173) sts.
Change to 3¾mm (US 5) circular needle.
Round 12: (K3, P1) 6 times, (K3, P2) 12 (12:
12: 13: 13: 13) times, (K3, P1) 6 times, (K3,
P2) 11 (12: 12: 12: 12: 12) times.
Rounds 13 and 14: As round 12.
Cast off in rib.
Join side and sleeve seams. Neatly sew cast-on
edge of pocket back in place on inside.

Recommendation

Suitable for the knitter with a little experience
Please see pages 32 & 33 for photographs.

	XS	S	M	L	XL	XXL	
To fit	**81**	**86**	**91**	**97**	**102**	**109**	cm
bust	32	34	36	38	40	43	in

Rowan Baby Alpaca DK

| | 12 | 13 | 14 | 14 | 15 | 16 | x 50gm |

Photographed in Lincoln

Needles

1 pair 2¾mm (no 12) (US 2) needles
1 pair 3mm (no 11) (US 2/3) needles
1 pair 3¼mm (no 10) (US 3) needles

Buttons - 19

Tension

24 sts and 33 rows to 10 cm measured over
stocking stitch using 3¼mm (US 3) needles.

WALLACE
TAILORED JACKET WITH BUTTONED POCKETS & CUFFS

BACK

Cast on 103 (109: 115: 121: 127: 137) sts
using 2¾mm (US 2) needles.
Beg with a K row, work in st st for 9 rows,
ending with a **RS** row.
Row 10 (picot row) (WS): *P2tog, yrn, rep
from * to last st, P1.
Change to 3¼mm (US 3) needles.
Beg with a K row, work in st st for 18 rows,
ending with a WS row.
Next row (dec) (RS): K3, K2tog, K to last 5 sts,
K2tog tbl, K3.
Working all side seam decreases as set by
last row, dec 1 st at each end of 8th and
3 foll 8th rows.
93 (99: 105: 111: 117: 127) sts.
Work 17 rows, ending with a WS row.
Next row (inc) (RS): K3, M1, K to last 3 sts,
M1, K3.
Working all side seam increases as set by last
row, inc 1 st at each end of 12th and 3 foll
12th rows.
103 (109: 115: 121: 127: 137) sts.
Cont straight until back measures 39 (39: 40:
40: 40: 40) cm **from picot row,** ending with
a WS row.
Shape armholes
Cast off 3 (4: 4: 5: 5: 6) sts at beg of next
2 rows.
97 (101: 107: 111: 117: 125) sts.
Dec 1 st at each end of next 5 (7: 7: 9: 9: 11)
rows, then on foll 2 (1: 3: 2: 4: 4) alt rows,
then on 2 foll 4th rows.
79 (81: 83: 85: 87: 91) sts.
Cont straight until armhole measures 18 (19:
19: 20: 21: 22) cm, ending with a WS row.
Shape shoulders and back neck
Cast off 8 (8: 8: 8: 8: 9) sts at beg of next
2 rows. 63 (65: 67: 69: 71: 73) sts.
Next row (RS): Cast off 8 (8: 8: 8: 8: 9) sts,
K until there are 11 (11: 12: 12: 13: 13) sts
on right needle and turn, leaving rem sts on
a holder.
Work each side of neck separately.
Cast off 4 sts at beg of next row.
Cast off rem 7 (7: 8: 8: 9: 9) sts.
With RS facing, rejoin yarn to rem sts, cast off
centre 25 (27: 27: 29: 29: 29) sts, K to end.
Complete to match first side, reversing
shapings.

LEFT FRONT

Cast on 53 (56: 59: 62: 65: 70) sts using
2¾mm (US 2) needles.
Beg with a K row, work in st st as folls:
Work 1 row.
Inc 1 st at beg of next row and at same edge
on foll 7 rows, ending with a RS row.
61 (64: 67: 70: 73: 78) sts.
Row 10 (picot row) (WS): Inc in first st, P1 (0:
1: 0: 1: 0), *P2tog, yrn, rep from * to last st,
P1. 62 (65: 68: 71: 74: 79) sts.
Change to 3¼mm (US 3) needles.
Place marker on 2nd st in from beg of last row.
Row 11 (RS): K to last 2 sts, sl marked st purlwise
(to form front opening edge fold line), inc in last st.
Row 12: Inc in first st, P to end.
64 (67: 70: 73: 76: 81) sts.
These 2 rows set the sts – all sts in st st with
marked st slipped purlwise on every RS row.
Cont as set, inc 1 st at front opening edge of
next 6 rows. 70 (73: 76: 79: 82: 87) sts, and
9 sts in st st at front opening edge beyond
slipped fold line st.
Working all side seam decreases as set by
back, dec 1 st at beg of 11th and 4 foll 8th
rows. 65 (68: 71: 74: 77: 82) sts.
Work 17 rows, ending with a WS row.
Working all side seam increases as set by
back, inc 1 st at beg of next and 4 foll 12th
rows. 70 (73: 76: 79: 82: 87) sts.
Cont straight until left front matches back to
beg of armhole shaping, ending with a WS row.
Shape armhole
Cast off 3 (4: 4: 5: 5: 6) sts at beg of next row.
67 (69: 72: 74: 77: 81) sts.
Work 1 row.
Dec 1 st at armhole edge of next 5 (7: 7: 9: 9:
11) rows, then on foll 2 (1: 3: 2: 4: 4) alt rows,
then on 2 foll 4th rows.
58 (59: 60: 61: 62: 64) sts.
Cont straight until 19 (19: 19: 21: 21: 21)
rows less have been worked than on back to
beg of shoulder shaping, ending with a **RS** row.
Shape neck
Cast off 22 (23: 23: 23: 23: 23) sts at beg
of next row. 36 (36: 37: 38: 39: 41) sts.
Dec 1 st at neck edge of next 9 rows, then
on foll 4 (4: 4: 5: 5: 5) alt rows.
23 (23: 24: 24: 25: 27) sts.
Work 1 row, ending with a WS row.

Shape shoulder

Cast off 8 (8: 8: 8: 8: 9) sts at beg of next and foll alt row.

Work 1 row.

Cast off rem 7 (7: 8: 8: 9: 9) sts.

Mark positions for 7 buttons along left front opening edge – first to come in row 17, last to come 2 cm below beg of front neck shaping, and rem 5 buttons evenly spaced between.

RIGHT FRONT

Cast on 53 (56: 59: 62: 65: 70) sts using 2¾mm (US 2) needles.

Beg with a K row, work in st st as folls:

Work 1 row.

Inc 1 st at end of next row and at same edge on foll 7 rows, ending with a **RS** row.

61 (64: 67: 70: 73: 78) sts.

Row 10 (picot row) (WS): *P2tog, yrn, rep from * to last 1 (2: 1: 2: 1: 2) sts, P0 (1: 0: 1: 0: 1), inc in last st.

62 (65: 68: 71: 74: 79) sts.

Change to 3¼mm (US 3) needles.

Place marker on 2nd st in from end of last row.

Row 11 (RS): Inc in first st, sl marked st purlwise (to form front opening edge fold line), K to end.

Row 12: P to last st, inc in last st.

64 (67: 70: 73: 76: 81) sts.

These 2 rows set the sts – all sts in st st with marked st slipped purlwise on every RS row.

Cont as set, inc 1 st at front opening edge of next 4 rows.

68 (71: 74: 77: 80: 85) sts.

Row 17 (first buttonhole row) (RS): K1, cast off **2** sts, K to marked st, sl marked st purlwise, K4, cast off 3 sts, K to end.

Row 18: P to last st, casting on 3 sts over **both** sets of cast-off sts, inc in last st.

70 (73: 76: 79: 82: 87) sts, and 9 sts in st st at front opening edge beyond slipped fold line st.

Working all side seam decreases as set by back, dec 1 st at end of 11th row.

Complete to match left front, reversing shapings and working a further 6 buttonholes to correspond with positions marked for buttons as folls:

Buttonhole row (RS): K2, cast off 3 sts (to make first buttonhole of this pair – cast on 3 sts over these cast-off sts on next row), K to marked st, sl marked st purlwise, K4, cast off 3 sts (to make 2nd buttonhole of this pair – cast on 3 sts over these cast-off sts on next row), K to end.

LEFT SLEEVE

Front sleeve

Cast on 37 (38: 39: 40: 42: 43) sts using 3¼mm (US 3) needles.

Row 1 (RS): (K1, P1) twice, K to end.

Row 2: P to last 5 sts, (K1, P1) twice, K1.

These 2 rows set the sts – cuff opening edge 5 sts in moss st with all other sts in st st.

Working all sleeve increases in same way as side seam increases, cont as set, shaping sleeve by inc 1 st at end of 9th (9th: 9th: 9th: 11th: 9th) row.

38 (39: 40: 41: 43: 44) sts.

Work 7 (7: 7: 7: 5: 7) rows, ending with a WS row.

Break yarn and leave sts on a holder.

Back sleeve

Cast on 17 (18: 19: 20: 22: 23) sts using 3¼mm (US 3) needles.

Row 1 (RS): K to last 4 sts, (P1, K1) twice.

Row 2: (K1, P1) twice, K1, P to end.

These 2 rows set the sts – cuff opening edge 5 sts in moss st with all other sts in st st.

Working all sleeve increases in same way as side seam increases, cont as set, shaping sleeve by inc 1 st at beg of 9th (9th: 9th: 9th: 11th: 9th) row. 18 (19: 20: 21: 23: 24) sts.

Work 7 (7: 7: 7: 5: 7) rows, ending with a WS row.

Join sections

Next row (RS): K to last 5 sts of back sleeve, holding WS of front sleeve against RS of back sleeve, K tog first st of front sleeve with next st of back sleeve, (K tog next st of front sleeve with next st of back sleeve) 4 times, K to end.

51 (53: 55: 57: 61: 63) sts.

**Now working all sts in st st beg with a P row, cont as folls:

Inc 1 st at each end of 2nd (2nd: 2nd: 2nd: 6th: 2nd) and every foll 10th (10th: 12th: 10th: 12th: 10th) row to 59 (69: 75: 67: 77: 67) sts, then on every foll 12th (12th: -: 12th: 14th: 12th) row until there are 71 (75: -: 79: 81: 85) sts.

Cont straight until sleeve measures 42 (43: 44: 45: 46: 47) cm, ending with a WS row.

Shape top

Cast off 3 (4: 4: 5: 5: 6) sts at beg of next 2 rows. 65 (67: 67: 69: 71: 73) sts.

Dec 1 st at each end of next 3 rows, then on foll alt row, then on 6 foll 4th rows.

45 (47: 47: 49: 51: 53) sts.

Work 1 row, ending with a WS row.

Dec 1 st at each end of next and every foll alt row to 39 sts, then on foll 5 rows, ending with a WS row.

Cast off rem 29 sts.

RIGHT SLEEVE

Back sleeve

Cast on 17 (18: 19: 20: 22: 23) sts using 3¼mm (US 3) needles.

Row 1 (RS): (K1, P1) twice, K to end.

Row 2: P to last 5 sts, (K1, P1) twice, K1.

These 2 rows set the sts – cuff opening edge 5 sts in moss st with all other sts in st st.

Working all sleeve increases in same way as side seam increases, cont as set, shaping sleeve by inc 1 st at end of 9th (9th: 9th: 9th: 11th: 9th) row.

18 (19: 20: 21: 23: 24) sts.

Work 7 (7: 7: 7: 5: 7) rows, ending with a WS row.

Break yarn and leave sts on a holder.

Front sleeve

Cast on 37 (38: 39: 40: 42: 43) sts using 3¼mm (US 3) needles.

Row 1 (RS): K to last 4 sts, (P1, K1) twice.

Row 2: (K1, P1) twice, K1, P to end.

These 2 rows set the sts – cuff opening edge 5 sts in moss st with all other sts in st st.

Working all sleeve increases in same way as side seam increases, cont as set, shaping sleeve by inc 1 st at beg of 9th (9th: 9th: 9th: 11th: 9th) row.

38 (39: 40: 41: 43: 44) sts.

Work 7 (7: 7: 7: 5: 7) rows, ending with a WS row.

Join sections

Next row (RS): K to last 5 sts of front sleeve, holding WS of front sleeve against RS of back sleeve, K tog next st of front sleeve with first st of back sleeve, (K tog next st of front sleeve with next st of back sleeve) 4 times, K to end. 51 (53: 55: 57: 61: 63) sts.

Complete as given for left sleeve from **.

MAKING UP

Pin the pieces out and steam gently without allowing the iron to touch the yarn.

Join both shoulder seams using back stitch or mattress stitch if preferred.

Collar

Cast on 105 (109: 109: 115: 115: 115) sts using 3mm (US 2/3) needles.

Row 1 (RS): K1, *P1, K1, rep from * to end.

Row 2: As row 1.

These 2 rows form moss st.

Work in moss st for a further 2 rows, ending with a WS row.

Row 5 (RS): Moss st 3 sts, cast off 2 sts (to make 8th buttonhole – cast on 2 sts over these cast-off sts on next row), moss st to end.

Work 3 rows, ending with a WS row.

Now shape collar as folls:

Row 1 (RS): Cast off 5 sts, moss st to last 34 (35: 35: 37: 37: 37) sts, wrap next st (by slipping next st on left needle onto right needle, taking yarn to opposite side of work between needles and then slipping same st back onto left needle – when working back across wrapped sts, work the wrapped st and the wrapping loop tog as one st) and turn.

Row 2: Moss st 37 (39: 39: 41: 41: 41) sts, wrap next st and turn.

Row 3: Moss st 43 (45: 45: 47: 47: 47) sts, wrap next st and turn.

Row 4: Moss st 49 (51: 51: 53: 53: 53) sts, wrap next st and turn.

Row 5: Moss st 55 (57: 57: 59: 59: 59) sts, wrap next st and turn.

Row 6: Moss st 61 (63: 63: 65: 65: 65) sts, wrap next st and turn.

Row 7: Moss st to end.

Row 8: Cast off 5 sts, moss st to end.
95 (99: 99: 105: 105: 105) sts.
Work 4 rows, ending with a WS row.

Next row (inc) (RS): Moss st 3 sts, inc twice in next st as folls: K into front loop, P into back loop, then K into front loop again – 2 sts increased, moss st to last 4 sts, inc twice in next st, moss st 3 sts.
Work 3 rows.
Rep last 4 rows 5 times more, then first of these rows (the inc row) again.
123 (127: 127: 133: 133: 133) sts.
Work 1 row, ending with a WS row.
Cast off in moss st.
Fold front opening edges to inside along fold line sts and neatly sew in place.
Sew cast-on edge of collar to neck edge, matching ends of collar cast-on edge to fold lines of fronts.

Lower pockets (make 2)
Cast on 27 (27: 29: 29: 31: 31) sts using 3¼mm (US 3) needles.
Work in moss st as given for collar for 4 rows, ending with a WS row.

Row 5: Moss st 4 sts, P to last 4 sts, moss st 4 sts.

Row 6: Moss st 4 sts, K to last 4 sts, moss st 4 sts.
Rep last 2 rows 5 times more.

Row 17 (RS): K2, M1, K to last 2 sts, M1, K2.
29 (29: 31: 31: 33: 33) sts.
Beg with a P row, work in st st for 27 rows, ending with a WS row.
Dec 1 st at each end of next 4 rows, ending with a WS row.
Cast off rem 21 (21: 23: 23: 25: 25) sts.

Upper pockets (make 2)
Cast on 23 (23: 25: 25: 27: 27) sts using 3¼mm (US 3) needles.
Work in moss st as given for collar for 4 rows, ending with a WS row.

Row 5: Moss st 4 sts, P to last 4 sts, moss st 4 sts.

Row 6: Moss st 4 sts, K to last 4 sts, moss st 4 sts.
Rep last 2 rows 5 times more.

Row 17 (RS): K2, M1, K to last 2 sts, M1, K2.
25 (25: 27: 27: 29: 29) sts.
Beg with a P row, work in st st for 21 rows, ending with a WS row.
Dec 1 st at each end of next 4 rows, ending with a WS row.
Cast off rem 17 (17: 19: 19: 21: 21) sts.
Join side seams.
Fold cast-on edge to inside along picot row and neatly sew in place. Fold first 16 rows of pockets over onto RS of rest of pocket and secure in place by attaching 2 buttons through both layers as in photograph. Using photograph as a guide, sew pockets onto fronts.
Join sleeve seams.

Cuffs (both alike)
Cast on 23 sts using 3¼mm (US 3) needles.
Row 1 (RS): K1, (sl next st purlwise, K9) twice, sl next st purlwise, K1.
Row 2: Purl.
These 2 rows set the sts – 3 slipped st fold lines and rem sts in st st.
Cont as set for a further 2 rows.
Row 5 (buttonhole row) (RS): Patt 6 sts, cast off 2 sts (to make first buttonhole of this pair – cast on 2 sts over these cast-off sts on next row), patt until there are 7 sts on right needle after cast-off, cast off 2 sts (to make 2nd buttonhole of this pair – cast on 2 sts over these cast-off sts on next row), patt to end.
Cont as set until row-end edge of cuff fits neatly around lower edge of sleeve, ending with a WS row.
Cast off.
Sew one row-end edge of cuff to lower edge of sleeve, positioning buttonhole end of cuff at opening edge of front sleeve. Fold cuff in half to inside and neatly sew in place.
Insert sleeves into armholes. Sew on buttons, attaching 8 buttons along left front opening edge to correspond with buttonholes, and one to each cuff to correspond with buttonhole.
Fold collar so that cast-off edge matches neck seam at centre back and attach last button through both layers at centre back to secure collar in place.

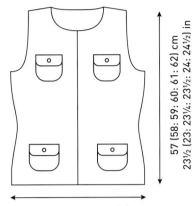

57 (58: 59: 60: 61: 62) cm
23½ (23: 23¼: 23½: 24: 24½) in

43 (45.5: 48: 50.5: 53: 57) cm
17 (18: 19: 20: 21: 22½) in

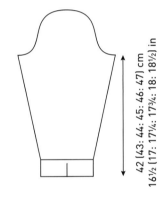

42 (43: 44: 45: 46: 47) cm
16½ (17: 17¼: 17¾: 18: 18½) in

NELLIE

COSY SWEATER WITH GENEROUS RAGLAN SLEEVES

Recommendation

Suitable for a novice knitter

Please see pages 28, 29 & 30 for photographs.

	XS	S	M	L	XL	XXL	
To fit	81	86	91	97	102	109	cm
bust	32	34	36	38	40	43	in

Rowan Alpaca Cotton

6   7   7   7   8   8   x 50gm

Photographed in Storm

Needles

1 pair 4mm (no 8) (US 6) needles
1 pair 4½mm (no 7) (US 7) needles
1 pair 6mm (no 4) (US 10) needles
1 pair 7mm (no 2) (US 10½) needles

Tension

13½ sts and 18 rows to 10 cm measured over stocking stitch using 7mm (US 10½) needles.
20 sts and 29 rows to 10 cm measured over stocking stitch using 4mm (US 6) needles.

BACK

Cast on 75 (79: 83: 85: 89: 95) sts using 4mm (US 6) needles.
Beg with a K row, work in st st as folls:
Work 10 rows, ending with a WS row.
Row 11 (RS): K3, K2tog, K to last 5 sts, K2tog tbl, K3.
Work 9 rows.
Rep last 10 rows once more, ending with a WS row. 71 (75: 79: 81: 85: 91) sts.
Change to 7mm (US 10½) needles.
Cont straight until back measures 38 (38: 39: 39: 39: 39) cm, ending with a WS row.
Shape raglan armholes
Cast off 4 sts at beg of next 2 rows.
63 (67: 71: 73: 77: 83) sts.
Work 2 rows.
Next row (RS): K1, K2tog, K to last 3 sts, K2tog tbl, K1.
Working all raglan armhole decreases as set by last row, dec 1 st at each end of 4th (4th: 4th: 4th: 4th: 2nd) and 3 (3: 1: 2: 1: 0) foll 4th rows, then on foll 16 (17: 21: 20: 23: 27) alt rows.
21 (23: 23: 25: 25: 25) sts.
Work 1 row, ending with a WS row.
Cast off.

FRONT

Work as given for back until 55 (57: 57: 61: 61: 61) sts rem in raglan armhole shaping.
Work 3 (1: 1: 1: 1: 1) rows, ending with a WS row.
Divide for neck
Next row (RS): K1, K2tog, K24 (25: 25: 27: 27: 27) and turn, leaving rem sts on a holder.
Work each side of neck separately.
Now working raglan armhole decreases as set and neck decreases in same way, cont as folls:
Dec 1 st at raglan armhole edge of 2nd and foll 10 (10: 10: 11: 11: 11) alt rows **and at same time** dec 1 st at neck edge of 2nd and foll 9 (10: 10: 11: 11: 11) alt rows. 5 sts.
Work 1 row, ending with a WS row.
Next row (RS): K1, K3tog, K1.
Next row: P3.
Next row: K1, K2tog.
Next row: P2.
Next row: K2tog and fasten off.
With RS facing, rejoin yarn to rem sts, K2tog, K to last 3 sts, K2tog tbl, K1.
Complete to match first side, reversing shapings.

SLEEVES

Main section

Cast on 71 (73: 73: 75: 77: 79) sts using 7mm (US 10½) needles.
Beg with a K row, work in st st until sleeve measures 27 (28: 29: 30: 31: 32) cm, ending with a WS row.
Shape raglan
Cast off 4 sts at beg of next 2 rows.
63 (65: 65: 67: 69: 71) sts.
Working raglan decreases in same way as raglan armhole decreases, dec 1 st at each end of next and every foll alt row until 17 sts rem.
Work 1 row, ending with a WS row.
Left sleeve only
Dec 1 st at each end of next row, then cast off 3 sts at beg of foll row. 12 sts.
Dec 1 st at beg of next row, then cast off 3 sts at beg of foll row. 8 sts.
Right sleeve only
Cast off 4 sts at beg and dec 1 st at end of next row. 12 sts.
Work 1 row.
Cast off 3 sts at beg and dec 1 st at end of next row. 8 sts.
Work 1 row.
Both sleeves
Rep last 2 rows once more.
Cast off rem 4 sts.
Cuff
With RS facing and using 4½mm (US 7) needles, pick up and knit 71 (73: 73: 75: 77: 79) sts from cast-on edge.
Row 1 (WS): (P1, P2tog) 2 (1: 5: 4: 7: 6) times, (P2tog) 28 (32: 20: 24: 16: 20) times, (P2tog, P1) 3 (2: 6: 5: 8: 7) times.
38 (38: 42: 42: 46: 46) sts.
Row 2: K2, *P2, K2, rep from * to end.
Row 3: P2, *K2, P2, rep from * to end.
These 2 rows form rib.
Cont in rib until cuff measures 8 cm from pick-up row, ending with a WS row.
Cast off in rib.

MAKING UP

Pin the pieces out and steam gently without allowing the iron to touch the yarn.
Join both front and right back raglan seams using back stitch or mattress stitch if preferred.

Neckband

With RS facing and using 6mm (US 10) needles, pick up and knit 12 sts from top of left sleeve, 26 (26: 26: 28: 28: 28) sts down left side of neck, 26 (26: 26: 28: 28: 28) sts up right side of neck, 12 sts from top of right sleeve, then 19 (21: 21: 23: 23: 23) sts from back. 95 (97: 97: 103: 103: 103) sts.

Cast off knitwise (on **WS**).

Join left back raglan and neckband seam. Join side and sleeve seams.

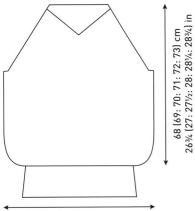

68 (69: 70: 71: 72: 73) cm
26¾ (27: 27½: 28: 28¼: 28¾) in

52.5 (55.5: 58.8: 60: 63: 67.5) cm
20¾ (21¾: 22¾: 23¾: 24¾: 26½) in

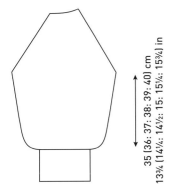

35 (36: 37: 38: 39: 40) cm
13¾ (14¼: 14½: 15: 15¼: 15¾) in

Recommendation

Suitable for the knitter with a little experience
Please see pages 26, 29 & 31 for photographs.

	S	M	L	XL	
To fit	97	102	107	112	cm
chest	38	40	42	44	in

Rowan Felted Tweed Aran

	13	13	14	15	x 50gm

Photographed in Soot & Dusty

Needles

1 pair 4½mm (no 7) (US 7) needles
1 pair 5mm (no 6) (US 8) needles

Tension

17 sts and 23 rows to 10 cm measured over
rib **when lightly pressed** using 5mm (US 8)
needles.

VICTOR
RUGGED RIBBED SWEATER

BACK

Cast on 93 (97: 101: 107) sts using 4½mm
(US 7) needles.
Row 1 (RS): K0 (0: 3: 0), P4 (6: 5: 6), *K5, P5,
rep from * to last 9 (1: 3: 1) sts, K5 (0: 3: 0),
P4 (1: 0: 1).
Row 2: P0 (0: 3: 0), K4 (6: 5: 6), *P5, K5,
rep from * to last 9 (1: 3: 1) sts, P5 (0: 3: 0),
K4 (1: 0: 1).
These 2 rows form rib.
Cont in rib for a further 4 rows, ending with a
WS row.
Change to 5mm (US 8) needles.
Cont in rib until back measures 45 cm, ending
with a WS row.
Shape armholes
Keeping rib correct, cast off 3 (4: 4: 5) sts at
beg of next 2 rows. 87 (89: 93: 97) sts.
Next row (RS): P1 (2: 4: 1), K5, P2tog, patt to
last 8 (9: 11: 8) sts, P2tog tbl, K5, P1 (2: 4: 1).
Next row: K1 (2: 4: 1), P5, K1, patt to last 7 (8:
10: 7) sts, K1, P5, K1 (2: 4: 1).
Rep last 2 rows 9 times more.
67 (69: 73: 77) sts.
Cont straight until armhole measures 21 (22:
23: 24) cm, ending with a WS row.
Shape shoulders and back neck
Cast off 5 (5: 5: 6) sts at beg of next 4 rows,
then 5 (5: 6: 5) sts at beg of foll 2 rows.
Cast off rem 37 (39: 41: 43) sts.

FRONT

Work as given for back until 6 rows less have
been worked than on back to beg of shoulder
shaping, ending with a WS row.
Shape front neck
Next row (RS): Patt 19 (19: 20: 21) sts and
turn, leaving rem sts on a holder.
Work each side of neck separately.
Keeping patt correct, dec 1 st at neck edge
of next 2 rows, then on foll alt row.
16 (16: 17: 18) sts.
Work 1 row, ending with a WS row.
Shape shoulder
Cast off 5 (5: 5: 6) sts at beg and dec 1 st
at end of next row.
Work 1 row.
Cast off 5 (5: 5: 6) sts at beg of next row.
Work 1 row.
Cast off rem 5 (5: 6: 5) sts.

With RS facing, slip centre 29 (31: 33: 35) sts
onto a holder, rejoin yarn to rem sts, patt to end.
Complete to match first side, reversing
shapings.

SLEEVES (both alike)

Cast on 47 (49: 51: 53) sts using
4½mm (US 7) needles.
Row 1 (RS): P1 (2: 3: 4), K5, *P5, K5, rep from
* to last 1 (2: 3: 4) sts, P1 (2: 3: 4).
Row 2: K1 (2: 3: 4), P5, *K5, P5, rep from * to
last 1 (2: 3: 4) sts, K1 (2: 3: 4).
These 2 rows form rib.
Cont in rib for a further 4 rows, ending with
a WS row.
Change to 5mm (US 8) needles.
Cont in rib for a further 23 rows, inc 1 st at
each end of 11th row and ending with a **RS**
row. 49 (51: 53: 55) sts.
Cast off in patt (on **WS**).
With **WS** facing (so that ridge is formed on RS
of sleeve) and using 5mm (US 8) needles, pick
up and knit 49 (51: 53: 55) sts along cast-off
edge.
Next row (RS): Inc in first st, P1 (2: 3: 4), K5,
*P5, K5, rep from * to last 2 (3: 4: 5) sts, P1
(2: 3: 4), inc in last st. 51 (53: 55: 57) sts.
Keeping sts correct as set by last row, cont in
rib, shaping sides by inc 1 st at each end of
18th and 3 foll 18th rows, taking inc sts into
rib. 59 (61: 63: 65) sts.
Cont straight until sleeve measures 51 (52:
53: 54) cm, ending with a WS row.
Shape top
Keeping rib correct, cast off 3 (4: 4: 5) sts at
beg of next 2 rows. 53 (53: 55: 55) sts.
Dec 1 st at each end of next 3 rows, then on
foll alt row, then on 3 (4: 4: 5) foll 4th rows.
39 (37: 39: 37) sts.
Work 1 row.
Dec 1 st at each end of next and foll 3 (2: 3: 2)
alt rows, then on foll 5 rows, ending with
a WS row.
Cast off rem 21 sts.

MAKING UP

Pin the pieces out and steam gently without
allowing the iron to touch the yarn.
Join right shoulder seam using back stitch
or mattress stitch if preferred.

Neckband

With RS facing and using 4½mm (US 7) needles, pick up and knit 10 sts down left side of neck, patt across 29 (31: 33: 35) sts on front holder, pick up and knit 10 sts up right side of neck, then 37 (39: 41: 43) sts from back. 86 (90: 94: 98) sts.

Row 1 (WS): P1 (2: 3: 0), (K4, P5) 0 (0: 0: 1) time, (K5, P5) 3 times, K5 (5: 5: 4), P8 (10: 4: 5), (K4, P4) 0 (0: 1: 0) times, (K5, P5) 3 (3: 3: 4) times, (K5, P4) 0 (0: 1: 0) times, K5 (5: 4: 5), P7 (8: 1: 5).

Row 2: K7 (8: 1: 5), P5 (5: 4: 5), (K4, P5) 0 (0: 1: 0) times, (K5, P5) 3 (3: 3: 4) times, (K4, P4) 0 (0: 1: 0) times, K8 (10: 4: 5), P5 (5: 5: 4), (K5, P5) 3 times, (K5, P4) 0 (0: 0: 1) time, K1 (2: 3: 0).

Rep last 2 rows 5 times more, ending with a **RS** row.

Cast off in patt (on **WS**).

Join left shoulder and neckband seam. Join side seams. Join sleeve seams. Insert sleeves into armholes.

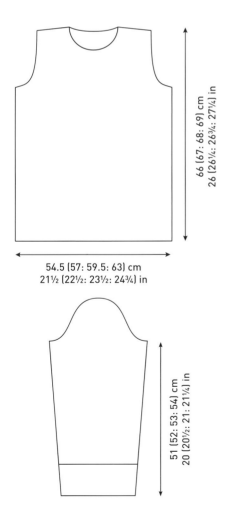

66 (67: 68: 69) cm
26 (26¼: 26¾: 27¼) in

54.5 (57: 59.5: 63) cm
21½ (22½: 23½: 24¾) in

51 (52: 53: 54) cm
20 (20½: 21: 21¼) in

ELEANOR

SUMPTUOUS BLOUSY SWEATER WITH GRACEFUL NECKLINE

Recommendation
Suitable for the knitter with a little experience
Please see pages 40 & 41 for photographs.

	XS	S	M	L	XL	XXL	
To fit	**81**	**86**	**91**	**97**	**102**	**109**	cm
bust	32	34	36	38	40	43	in

Rowan Kidsilk Aura
    9   10   10   11   11   12   x 25gm
Photographed in Wheat

Needles
1 pair 3¾mm (no 9) (US 5) needles
1 pair 4½mm (no 7) (US 7) needles
1 pair 5½mm (no 5) (US 9) needles

Buttons - 10

Tension
15 sts and 20 rows to 10 cm measured over
stocking stitch using 5½mm (US 9) needles.
21 sts and 29 rows to 10 cm measured over
stocking stitch using 3¾mm (US 5) needles.

Pattern note: Sweater is knitted from top
downwards, beg at neck edge, increasing out
to underarm point, and then working down
towards hem edge.

BACK and FRONT (both alike – worked downwards)
Cast on 43 (45: 45: 47: 47: 47) sts using 5½mm (US 9) needles.
Beg with a K row, work in st st and shape neck as folls:
Row 1 (RS): K4, wrap next st (by slipping next st on left needle onto right needle, taking yarn to opposite side of work between needles and then slipping same st back onto left needle – when working back across wrapped sts, work the wrapped st and the wrapping loop tog as one st) and turn.
Row 2: Purl.
Row 3: K3, M1, K4, wrap next st and turn.
Row 4: Purl.
Row 5: K3, M1, K8, wrap next st and turn.
Row 6: Purl.
Row 7: K3, M1, K to end.
Row 8: P4, wrap next st and turn.
Row 9: K1, M1, K3.
Row 10: P8, wrap next st and turn.
Row 11: K5, M1, K3.
Row 12: P12, wrap next st and turn.
Row 13: K9, M1, K3.
Row 14: Purl across all sts.
49 (51: 51: 53: 53: 53) sts.
These 14 rows complete neck shaping.
Next row (RS): K3, M1, K to last 3 sts, M1, K3.
Next row: Purl.
Rep last 2 rows 4 (5: 3: 4: 4: 3) times more.
59 (63: 59: 63: 63: 61) sts.
Sizes M, L, XL and XXL only
Next row (RS): K3, M1, K to last 3 sts, M1, K3.
Next row: P3, M1, P to last 3 sts, M1, P3.
Rep last 2 rows – (-: 1: 1: 2: 4) times more.
- (-: 67: 71: 75: 81) sts.
All sizes
Cast on 5 sts at beg of next 2 rows.
69 (73: 77: 81: 85: 91) sts.
Place markers at both ends of last row to denote underarm point.
Cont straight until work measures 41 (41: 42: 42: 42: 42) cm from markers, ending with a WS row.
Change to 3¾mm (US 5) needles.
Work 10 rows, ending with a WS row.
Next row (RS): K3, M1, K to last 3 sts, M1, K3.
Work 11 rows.

Rep last 12 rows twice more, ending with a WS row. 75 (79: 83: 87: 91: 97) sts.
Cast off.

SLEEVES (worked downwards)
Cast on 30 sts using 5½mm (US 9) needles.
Beg with a K row, work in st st as folls:
Work 2 rows, ending with a WS row.
Next row (RS): K3, M1, K to last 3 sts, M1, K3.
Next row: Purl.
Rep last 2 rows 7 (8: 8: 9: 10: 11) times more.
46 (48: 48: 50: 52: 54) sts.
Cast on 5 sts at beg of next 2 rows.
56 (58: 58: 60: 62: 64) sts.
Place markers at both ends of last row to denote underarm point.
Working all increases as set by armhole increases, inc 1 st at each end of 7th and 2 foll 8th rows. 62 (64: 64: 66: 68: 70) sts.
Cont straight until sleeve measures 21 (22: 23: 24: 25: 26) cm from markers, ending with a WS row.
Change to 3¾mm (US 5) needles.
Next row (RS): K3 (0: 0: 1: 2: 3), (K1, K2tog, K1) 14 (16: 16: 16: 16: 16) times, K3 (0: 0: 1: 2: 3). 48 (48: 48: 50: 52: 54) sts.
Next row: Purl.
Next row: (K1, K2tog) 4 (3: 2: 2: 2: 2) times, K to last 12 (9: 6: 6: 6: 6) sts, (K2tog, K1) 4 (3: 2: 2: 2: 2) times. 40 (42: 44: 46: 48: 50) sts.
Work 19 rows, ending with a WS row.
Next row (RS): K3, K2tog, K to last 5 sts, K2tog tbl, K3.
Working all decreases as set by last row, dec 1 st at each end of 20th row.
36 (38: 40: 42: 44: 46) sts.
Work 19 rows, ending with a WS row.
Divide for cuff opening
Left sleeve only
Next row (RS): K3, K2tog, K22 (23: 24: 25: 26: 27) and turn, leaving rem sts on a holder.
Work each side of cuff separately.
Next row (WS): K2, P to end.
Next row: Knit.
These 2 rows set the sts.
Cont as set for a further 17 rows, ending with a WS row.
Cast off.
With RS facing, rejoin yarn to rem sts, K2tog, K to last 5 sts, K2tog tbl, K3. 7 (8: 9: 10: 11: 12) sts.

Next row (WS): P to last 2 sts, K2.
Next row: Knit.
These 2 rows set the sts.
Cont as set for a further 17 rows, ending with a WS row.
Cast off.
Right sleeve only
Next row (RS): K3, K2tog, K3 (4: 5: 6: 7: 8) and turn, leaving rem sts on a holder.
Work each side of cuff separately.
Next row (WS): K2, P to end.
Next row: Knit.
These 2 rows set the sts.
Cont as set for a further 17 rows, ending with a WS row.
Cast off.
With RS facing, rejoin yarn to rem sts, K2tog, K to last 5 sts, K2tog tbl, K3.
26 (27: 28: 29: 30: 31) sts.
Next row (WS): P to last 2 sts, K2.
Next row: Knit.
These 2 rows set the sts.
Cont as set for a further 17 rows, ending with a WS row.
Cast off.

MAKING UP
Pin the pieces out and steam gently without allowing the iron to touch the yarn.
Join both front and right back raglan seams using back stitch or mattress stitch if preferred.
Neckband
With RS facing and using 4½mm (US 7) needles, pick up and knit 28 sts from top of left sleeve placing marker between centre 2 sts, place marker on right needle, pick up and knit 42 (44: 44: 46: 46: 46) sts from front, place marker on right needle, pick up and knit 28 sts from top of right sleeve placing marker between centre 2 sts, place marker on right needle, then pick up and knit 42 (44: 44: 46: 46: 46) sts from back.
140 (144: 144: 148: 148: 148) sts. 5 markers in total.
Row 1 (WS): Knit.
Row 2: K2, K2tog tbl, *K to within 4 sts of next marker, K2tog, K4 (marker is at centre of these sts), K2tog tbl, rep from * 4 times more, K to last 4 sts, K2tog, K2.
128 (132: 132: 136: 136: 136) sts.
Rows 3 to 5: Knit.
Rows 6 to 9: As rows 2 to 5. 116 (120: 120: 124: 124: 124) sts.
Row 10: As row 2. 104 (108: 108: 112: 112: 112) sts.
Cast off knitwise (on **WS**).

Join left back raglan and neckband seam. Join side and sleeve seams. Overlap cuff opening edges so that front g st section sits over back g st section and sew on buttons through both layers to secure cuff opening closed.

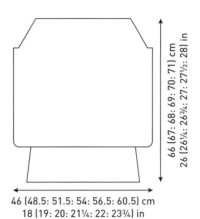

46 (48.5: 51.5: 54: 56.5: 60.5) cm
18 (19: 20: 21¼: 22: 23¾) in

66 (67: 68: 69: 70: 71) cm
26 (26¼: 26¾: 27: 27½: 28) in

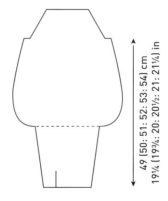

49 (50: 51: 52: 53: 54) cm
19¼ (19¾: 20: 20½: 21: 21¼) in

Recommendation

Suitable for the knitter with a little experience
Please see pages 42, 43 & 47 for photographs.

	XS	S	M	L	XL	XXL	
To fit	**81**	**86**	**91**	**97**	**102**	**109**	cm
bust	32	34	36	38	40	43	in

Rowan Drift or Big Wool

7   8   8   9   9   10 x 100gm
Photographed in Drift Sombre

Needles

1 pair 8mm (no 0) (US 11) needles
1 pair 10mm (no 000) (US 15) needles

Tension

9½ sts and 14 rows to 10 cm measured over
pattern using 10mm (US 15) needles.

Yarn note: Rowan Drift is **NOT** a solid coloured
yarn and the colour tones vary within each
ball. To ensure garment is an even tone
throughout, start each section at the same
point in the colour variation.

LOIS

SLOUCHY JACKET WITH A TOUCH OF THE BOHEMIAN

RIGHT SIDE

(knitted sideways, beg at cuff edge)
Cast on 40 (40: 40: 42: 42: 44) sts using
10mm (US 15) needles.
Work in g st for 10 rows, dec 1 st at each end
of 7th of these rows.
38 (38: 38: 40: 40: 42) sts.
Change to 8mm (US 11) needles.
Work in g st for a further 10 rows.
Change to 10mm (US 15) needles.
Work in g st for a further 2 rows, ending
with a WS row.
Now work in patt as folls:
Row 1 (RS): Inc in first st, K to last st, inc
in last st. 40 (40: 40: 42: 42: 44) sts.
Row 2: Purl.
Row 3: Knit.
Row 4: Purl.
Row 5: As row 1.
42 (42: 42: 44: 44: 46) sts.
Rows 6 and 7: Knit.
Row 8: Purl.
Row 9: As row 1.
44 (44: 44: 46: 46: 48) sts.
Row 10: Purl.
Rows 11 and 12: Knit.
Row 13: Inc in first st, P to last st, inc in last st.
46 (46: 46: 48: 48: 50) sts.
Row 14: Knit.
These 14 rows form patt and beg sleeve
shaping.
Cont in patt, shaping sides by inc 1 st at each
end of next (next: 3rd: 3rd: 3rd: 3rd) and 0 (0:
0: 0: 0: 1) foll 4th row, then on foll 1 (2: 2: 2:
3: 2) alt rows, then on foll 5 rows, ending with
a WS row.
60 (62: 62: 64: 66: 68) sts.
Right sleeve is now completed.
Shape side seam
Next row (RS): Cast on 25 (25: 26: 26: 26:
26) sts, work across these sts as folls: K4,
patt to end.
Next row: Cost on 25 (25: 26: 26: 26: 26) sts,
work across these sts as follows: K4, patt to last
4 sts, K4.
110 (112: 114: 116: 118: 120) sts.

Last 2 rows set the sts – first and last 4 sts
of every row now worked in g st with all other
sts still in patt.
Work 37 (39: 41: 41: 43: 45) rows, ending
with a **RS** row.**
Divide for back and front
Next row (WS): Patt 54 (55: 56: 57: 58: 59)
sts and slip these sts onto a holder for back,
cast off next 7 sts, patt to end.
49 (50: 51: 52: 53: 54) sts.
Work 1 row.
Cast on 10 (10: 10: 11: 11: 11) sts at beg
of next row (for back neck border extension).
59 (60: 61: 63: 64: 65) sts.
Work 1 (1: 1: 3: 3: 3) rows, ending with
a **RS** row.
Work in g st for 4 rows, ending with a **RS** row.
Cast off knitwise (on **WS**).
With RS facing, rejoin yarn to rem sts, patt
to end.
Dec 1 st at neck edge of 2nd row.
53 (54: 55: 56: 57: 58) sts.
Work a further 5 (5: 5: 7: 7: 7) rows, ending
with a WS row.
Break yarn and leave these sts on a holder.

LEFT SIDE

(knitted sideways, beg at cuff edge)
Work as given for right side to **.
Divide for back and front
Next row (WS): Patt 49 (50: 51: 52: 53: 54)
sts and slip these sts onto a holder for front,
cast off next 7 sts, patt to end.
54 (55: 56: 57: 58: 59) sts.
Dec 1 st at neck edge of 3rd row.
53 (54: 55: 56: 57: 58) sts.
Work a further 5 (5: 5: 7: 7: 7) rows, ending
with a WS row.
Break yarn and leave these sts on a holder.
With RS facing, rejoin yarn to rem sts, cast
on 10 (10: 10: 11: 11: 11) sts (for back neck
border extension), patt to end.
59 (60: 61: 63: 64: 65) sts.
Work 2 (2: 2: 4: 4: 4) rows, end with a **RS** row.
Work in g st for 4 rows, ending with a **RS** row.
Cast off knitwise (on **WS**).

MAKING UP

Pin the pieces out and steam gently without allowing the iron to touch the yarn.

Slip sts left on holders onto 10mm (US 15) needles and, holding pieces with **WS** tog (so that cast-off edge forms a ridge on RS), cast off both sets of sts tog, taking one st from first piece with corresponding st from second piece.

Join row-end edges of back neck border extensions, then sew one edge to back neck edge. Join side and sleeve seams, reversing seam for first 12 rows for turn-back cuff. Fold first 10 rows to RS and secure in place at seam.

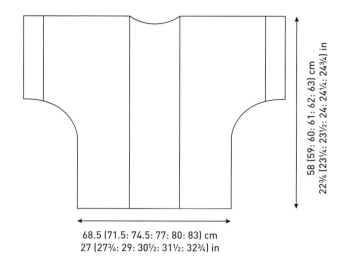

58 (59: 60: 61: 62: 63) cm
22¾ (23¼: 23¾: 24: 24¼: 24¾) in

68.5 (71.5: 74.5: 77: 80: 83) cm
27 (27¾: 29: 30½: 31½: 32¾) in

Recommendation

Suitable for the knitter with a little experience
Please see pages 34 & 50 for photographs.

	XS	S	M	L	XL	XXL	
To fit	**81**	**86**	**91**	**97**	**102**	**109**	**cm**
bust	32	34	36	38	40	43	in

Rowan Kidsilk Haze

| | 3 | 3 | 4 | 4 | 4 | 5 | x 25gm |

Photographed in Hurricane

Needles

1 pair 3¼mm (no 10) (US 3) needles

Tension

25 sts and 34 rows to 10 cm measured over
stocking stitch using 3¼mm (US 3) needles.

MAE
V-NECK VEST WITH CAPPED SLEEVES

BACK

Cast on 204 (216: 228: 240: 252: 272) sts
using 3¼mm (US 3) needles.

Row 1 (RS): *K2, lift 2nd st on right needle
over first st and off right needle, rep from * to
end. 102 (108: 114: 120: 126: 136) sts.

Beg with a P row, work in st st for 17 rows,
ending with a WS row.

Row 19 (dec) (RS): K3, K2tog, K to last 5 sts,
K2tog tbl, K3.

Working all side seam decreases as set by last
row, dec 1 st at each end of 8th and 4 foll 8th
rows. 90 (96: 102: 108: 114: 124) sts.

Work 19 (19: 23: 23: 23: 23) rows, ending
with a WS row.

Next row (inc) (RS): K3, M1, K to last 3 sts,
M1, K3.**

Working all side seam increases as set by last
row, inc 1 st at each end of 12th and 3 foll
12th rows.

100 (106: 112: 118: 124: 134) sts.

Work 9 rows, ending with a WS row. (Back
should measure 40 (40: 41: 41: 41: 41) cm.)

Shape armholes

Cast off 5 (7: 7: 8: 8: 9) sts at beg of next
2 rows. 90 (92: 98: 102: 108: 116) sts.

Next row (RS): K2, K2tog, K to last 4 sts,
K2tog tbl, K1, pick up loop lying between
needles and place this loop on right needle
(**note:** this loop does **NOT** count as a st), sl last
st purlwise.

Next row: P tog first st and the picked-up loop,
P1, P2tog tbl, P to last 4 sts, P2tog, P1, pick
up loop lying between needles and place this
loop on right needle (**note:** this loop does **NOT**
count as a st), sl last st knitwise.

Next row: K tog tbl first st and the picked-up
loop, K1, K2tog, K to last 4 sts, K2tog tbl, K1,
pick up loop lying between needles and place
this loop on right needle (**note:** this loop does
NOT count as a st), sl last st purlwise.

Next row: P tog first st and the picked-up loop,
P1, (P2tog tbl) 0 (0: 0: 0: 1: 1) times, P to last
2 (2: 2: 2: 4: 4) sts, (P2tog) 0 (0: 0: 0: 1: 1)
times, P1, pick up loop lying between needles
and place this loop on right needle (**note:**
this loop does **NOT** count as a st), sl last st
knitwise. 84 (86: 92: 96: 100: 108) sts.

Last 4 rows set the decreases and form slip
st edging.

Keeping slip st edging correct throughout and
working all armhole decreases as now set, cont
as folls:

Dec 1 st at each end of next and foll 0 (0: 0: 0:
1: 1) alt row, then on foll 4th row.

80 (82: 88: 92: 94: 102) sts.

Work 9 (9: 9: 11: 7: 9) rows, ending with
a WS row.

Next row (RS): K tog tbl first st and the
picked-up loop, K1, M1, K to last 2 sts, M1, K1,
pick up loop lying between needles and place
this loop on right needle (**note:** this loop does
NOT count as a st), sl last st purlwise.

Working all increases as set by last row, inc
1 st at each end of 4th and foll 10 (12: 12:
13: 15: 16) alt rows, then on foll 4th row.

106 (112: 118: 124: 130: 140) sts.

Work 7 rows, ending with RS facing for next
row.

Shape shoulders and back neck

Cast off 4 sts at beg of next 6 rows, 5 sts at
beg of foll 2 rows, and 7 (8: 9: 10: 11: 12) sts at
beg of next 2 rows.

58 (62: 66: 70: 74: 82) sts.

Next row (RS): Cast off 8 (8: 9: 10: 11: 13)
sts, K until there are 12 (13: 14: 14: 15: 17)
sts on right needle and turn, leaving rem sts
on a holder.

Work each side of neck separately.

Cast off 4 sts at beg of next row.

Cast off rem 8 (9: 10: 10: 11: 13) sts.

With RS facing, rejoin yarn to rem sts, cast off
centre 18 (20: 20: 22: 22: 22) sts, K to end.

Complete to match first side, reversing
shapings.

FRONT

Work as given for back to **.

Working all side seam increases as set by
last row, inc 1 st at each end of 12th and
foll 12th row.

96 (102: 108: 114: 120: 130) sts.

Work 5 rows, ending with RS facing for next row.

Divide for neck

Next row (RS): K44 (47: 50: 53: 56: 61),
K2tog tbl, K1, pick up loop lying between
needles and place this loop on right needle
(**note:** this loop does **NOT** count as a st), sl
next st purlwise and turn, leaving rem sts on
a holder.

Work each side of neck separately.
Now working slip st edging along neck slope and all neck decreases as set by last row, cont as folls:
Dec 1 st at neck edge of 6th and 3 foll 6th rows **and at same time** inc 1 st at side seam edge of 6th and foll 12th row.
45 (48: 51: 54: 57: 62) sts.
Work 3 rows, ending with a WS row.
Shape armhole
Cast off 5 (7: 7: 8: 8: 9) sts at beg of next row.
40 (41: 44: 46: 49: 53) sts.
Work 1 row.
Now working slip st edging along armhole edge and all armhole shaping as given for back, cont as folls:
Dec 1 st at armhole edge of next 3 (3: 3: 3: 5: 5) rows, then on foll alt row, then on foll 4th row **and at same time** dec 1 st at neck edge of next and foll 6th row.
33 (34: 37: 39: 40: 44) sts.
Dec 1 st at neck edge only on 4th (4th: 4th: 4th: 2nd: 2nd) and 0 (0: 0: 1: 0: 1) foll 6th row.
32 (33: 36: 37: 39: 42) sts.
Work 5 (5: 5: 1: 5: 1) rows, ending with a WS row.
Inc 1 st at armhole edge of next and foll 4th row, then on foll 10 (12: 12: 13: 15: 16) alt rows, then on foll 4th row **and at same time** dec 1 st at neck edge on next (next: next: 5th: next: 5th) and 0 (2: 2: 3: 3: 0) foll 6th rows, then on 3 (2: 2: 1: 2: 4) foll 8th rows.
41 (43: 46: 48: 51: 56) sts.
Work 7 rows, dec 1 st at neck edge of 4th of these rows and ending with RS facing for next row.
40 (42: 45: 47: 50: 55) sts.
Shape shoulder
Cast off 4 sts at beg of next and 2 foll alt rows, 5 sts at beg of foll alt row, 7 (8: 9: 10: 11: 12) sts at beg of foll alt row, then 8 (8: 9: 10: 11: 13) sts at beg of foll alt row.
Work 1 row.
Cast off rem 8 (9: 10: 10: 11: 13) sts.
With RS facing, rejoin yarn to rem sts, K2, K2tog, K to end.
Complete to match first side, reversing shapings.

MAKING UP
Pin the pieces out and steam gently without allowing the iron to touch the yarn.
Neckband
With RS facing and using 3¼mm (US 3) needles, pick up and knit 26 (28: 28: 30: 30: 30) sts across back neck.

Cast off knitwise (on **WS**), taking care not to cast off too tightly.
Join shoulder seams using back stitch or mattress stitch if preferred. Join side seams.

56 (58: 59: 60: 61: 62) cm
22 (22¾: 23¼: 23¾: 24: 24½) in

40 (42.5: 45: 47: 49.5: 53.5) cm
15¾ (16½: 17¾: 18½: 19¼: 21) in

NANCY
LONG-LINE DOUBLE BREASTED CARDIGAN

Recommendation
Suitable for the knitter with a little experience
Please see pages 38 & 39 for photographs.

	XS	S	M	L	XL	XXL	
To fit	81	86	91	97	102	109	cm
bust	32	34	36	38	40	43	in

Rowan Baby Alpaca DK
| 12 | 13 | 14 | 14 | 15 | 16 | x 50gm |

Photographed in Southdown

Needles
1 pair 3mm (no 11) (US 2/3) needles
1 pair 3¾mm (no 9) (US 5) needles

Buttons - 6

Tension
23 sts and 31 rows to 10 cm measured over
stocking stitch using 3¾mm (US 5) needles.

Special abbreviations
MP = make picot as folls: cast on 1 st, cast off
1 st – one st on right needle.

BACK
Cast on 111 (117: 123: 129: 135: 143) sts
using 3mm (US 2/3) needles.
Row 1 (RS): P0 (1: 0: 1: 0: 0), *K1, P1, rep
from * to last 1 (0: 1: 0: 1: 1) st, P1 (0: 1: 0:
1: 1).
Row 2: As row 1.
These 2 rows form moss st.
Cont in moss st for a further 6 rows, ending
with a WS row.
Change to 3¾mm (US 5) needles.
Beg with a K row, work in st st until back
measures 9 (9: 10: 10: 10: 10) cm, ending
with a WS row.
Next row (dec) (RS): K3, K2tog, K to last 5 sts,
K2tog tbl, K3.
Working all decreases as set by last row, dec
1 st at each end of 18th and 4 foll 18th rows.
99 (105: 111: 117: 123: 131) sts.
Work 55 rows, ending with a WS row. (Back
should measures 56 (56: 57: 57: 57: 57) cm.)
Shape armholes
Cast off 3 (4: 4: 5: 5: 6) sts at beg of next 2
rows. 93 (97: 103: 107: 113: 119) sts.
Dec 1 st at each end of next 5 (5: 7: 7: 9: 9)
rows, then on foll 2 (3: 3: 4: 4: 5) alt rows, then
on foll 4th row. 77 (79: 81: 83: 85: 89) sts.
Cont straight until armhole measures 18 (19:
19: 20: 21: 22) cm, ending with a WS row.
Shape shoulders and back neck
Cast off 7 (7: 7: 7: 7: 8) sts at beg of next 2
rows. 63 (65: 67: 69: 71: 73) sts.
Next row (RS): Cast off 7 (7: 7: 7: 7: 8) sts,
K until there are 10 (10: 11: 11: 12: 12) sts
on right needle and turn, leaving rem sts on
a holder.
Work each side of neck separately.
Cast off 4 sts at beg of next row.
Cast off rem 6 (6: 7: 7: 8: 8) sts.
With RS facing, rejoin yarn to rem sts, cast off
centre 29 (31: 31: 33: 33: 33) sts, K to end.
Complete to match first side, reversing
shapings.

LEFT FRONT
Cast on 71 (74: 77: 80: 83: 87) sts using
3mm (US 2/3) needles.
Row 1 (RS): P0 (1: 0: 1: 0: 0), *K1, P1, rep
from * to last 29 sts, K4, (P1, K1) 10 times,
P1, K4.

Row 2: MP, K until there are 4 sts on right
needle, (P1, K1) 10 times, P1, K4, *P1, K1, rep
from * to last 0 (1: 0: 1: 0: 0) st, P0 (1: 0: 1:
0: 0).
Row 3: As row 1.
Row 4: K4, (P1, K1) 10 times, P1, K4, *P1, K1,
rep from * to last 0 (1: 0: 1: 0: 0) st, P0 (1: 0:
1: 0: 0).
These 4 rows form patt.
Rep last 4 rows once more, ending with
a WS row.
Change to 3¾mm (US 5) needles.
Row 9 (RS): K to last 29 sts, patt to end.
Row 10: Patt 29 sts, P to end.
Last 2 rows set the sts – front opening edge
29 sts in g st and moss st with picot worked on
every 4th row and rem sts now worked in st st.
Cont as set until left front measures 9 (9: 10:
10: 10: 10) cm, ending with a WS row.
Working all side seam decreases as set by
back, dec 1 st at beg of next and 3 foll 18th
rows. 67 (70: 73: 76: 79: 83) sts.
Work 7 rows, ending with a WS row.
Shape front slope
Next row (RS): K to last 31 sts, K2tog tbl, patt
to end.
Working all front slope decreases as set by last
row, cont as folls:
Dec 1 st at front slope edge of 28th (22nd:
22nd: 20th: 22nd: 22nd) and 1 (2: 2: 3: 2: 2)
foll 28th (22nd: 22nd: 20th: 22nd: 22nd) rows
and at same time dec 1 st at side seam edge
of 10th and foll 18th row.
62 (64: 67: 69: 73: 77) sts.
Work 27 (17: 17: 3: 17: 17) rows, ending with
a WS row.
Shape armhole
Keeping sts correct, cast off 3 (4: 4: 5: 5: 6)
sts at beg and dec 1 (0: 0: 0: 0: 0) st at end
of next row. 58 (60: 63: 64: 68: 71) sts.
Work 1 row.
Dec 1 st at armhole edge of next 5 (5: 7: 7: 9:
9) rows, then on foll 2 (3: 3: 4: 4: 5) alt rows,
then on foll 4th row **and at same time** dec 1
st at front slope edge on 0 (3rd: 3rd: 15th:
3rd: 3rd) row. 50 (50: 51: 51: 53: 55) sts.
Work 8 (8: 6: 8: 10: 10) rows, dec 1 st at front
slope edge on 0 (0: 0: 0: 4th: 2nd) of these
rows and ending with a **RS** row.
50 (50: 51: 51: 52: 54) sts.

Next row (WS): Cast off 10 sts (for collar notch) then cast-on these 10 sts again, patt to end.

Dec 1 st at front slope edge of 5th (next: next: 7th: 15th: 13th) row.

49 (49: 50: 50: 51: 53) sts.

Cont straight until left front matches back to beg of shoulder shaping, ending with a WS row.

Shape shoulder

Cast off 7 (7: 7: 7: 7: 8) sts at beg of next and foll alt row, then 6 (6: 7: 7: 8: 8) sts at beg of foll alt row. 29 sts.

Cont in patt on these 29 sts only (for back collar extension) for a further 7.5 (8: 8: 8.5: 8.5: 8.5) cm, ending at outer (picot) edge of collar.

Next row: Patt 20 sts, wrap next st (by slipping next st on left needle onto right needle, taking yarn to opposite side of work between needles and then slipping same st back onto left needle – when working back across wrapped sts, work the wrapped st and the wrapping loop tog as one st) and turn.

Next row: Patt to end.

Next row: Patt 10 sts, wrap next st and turn.

Next row: Patt to end.

Cast off all 29 sts.

RIGHT FRONT

Cast on 71 (74: 77: 80: 83: 87) sts using 3mm (US 2/3) needles.

Row 1 (RS): MP, K until there are 4 sts on right needle, (P1, K1) 10 times, P1, K4, *P1, K1, rep from * to last 0 (1: 0: 1: 0: 0) st, P0 (1: 0: 1: 0: 0).

Row 2: P0 (1: 0: 1: 0: 0), *K1, P1, rep from * to last 29 sts, K4, (P1, K1) 10 times, P1, K4.

Row 3: K4, (P1, K1) 10 times, P1, K4, *P1, K1, rep from * to last 0 (1: 0: 1: 0: 0) st, P0 (1: 0: 1: 0: 0).

Row 4: As row 2.

These 4 rows form patt.

Rep last 4 rows once more, ending with a WS row.

Change to 3¾mm (US 5) needles.

Row 9 (RS): Patt 29 sts, K to end.

Row 10: P to last 29 sts, patt to end.

Last 2 rows set the sts – front opening edge 29 sts in g st and moss st with picot worked on every 4th row and rem sts now worked in st st.

Cont as set until right front measures 9 (9: 10: 10: 10: 10) cm, ending with a WS row.

Working all side seam decreases as set by back, dec 1 st at end of next row.

70 (73: 76: 79: 82: 86) sts.

Work 13 rows, ending with a WS row.

Next row (buttonhole row) (RS): Patt until there are 5 sts on right needle, cast off 3 sts (for first buttonhole of first pair of buttonholes – cast on 3 sts over these cast-off sts on next row), patt until there are 13 sts on right needle after cast-off, cast off 3 sts (for 2nd buttonhole of first pair of buttonholes – cast on 3 sts over these cast-off sts on next row), patt to end. Making a further 2 pairs of buttonholes in this way on 22nd and foll 22nd row and noting that no further reference will be made to buttonholes, cont as folls:

Dec 1 st at end of 4th and 2 foll 18th rows.

67 (70: 73: 76: 79: 83) sts.

Work 7 rows, ending with a WS row.

Shape front slope

Next row (RS): Patt 29 sts, K2tog, K to end.

Working all front slope decreases as set by last row, complete to match left front, reversing shapings.

SLEEVES (both alike)

Cast on 45 (47: 49: 51: 53: 55) sts using 3mm (US 2/3) needles.

Row 1 (RS): P1, *K1, P1, rep from * to end.

Row 2: As row 1.

These 2 rows form moss st.

Work in moss st for a further 6 rows, ending with a WS row.

Change to 3¾mm (US 5) needles.

Beg with a K row, work in st st for 4 rows, ending with a WS row.

Row 13 (inc) (RS): K3, M1, K to last 3 sts, M1, K3.

Working all increases as set by last row, inc 1 st at each end of 10th and 4 (8: 0: 5: 3: 8) foll 10th rows, then on every foll 12th row until there are 67 (71: 71: 75: 77: 81) sts.

Cont straight until sleeve measures 44 (45: 46: 47: 48: 49) cm, ending with a WS row.

Shape top

Cast off 3 (4: 4: 5: 5: 6) sts at beg of next 2 rows. 61 (63: 63: 65: 67: 69) sts.

Dec 1 st at each end of next 3 rows, then on foll alt row, then on 6 foll 4th rows.

41 (43: 43: 45: 47: 49) sts.

Work 1 row, ending with a WS row.

Dec 1 st at each end of next and every foll alt row to 35 sts, then on foll 5 rows, ending with a WS row.

Cast off rem 25 sts.

MAKING UP

Pin the pieces out and steam gently without allowing the iron to touch the yarn.

Join both shoulder seams using back stitch or mattress stitch if preferred. Join cast-off ends of back collar extensions, then sew one edge to back neck edge.

Join side seams. Join sleeve seams. Insert sleeves into armholes. Sew on buttons.

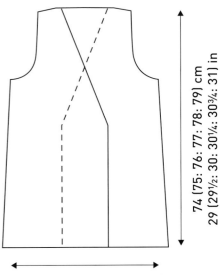

74 (75: 76: 77: 78: 79) cm
29 (29½: 30: 30½: 30¾: 31) in

43 (45.5: 48.5: 51: 53.5: 57) cm
17 (18: 19: 20: 21: 22½) in

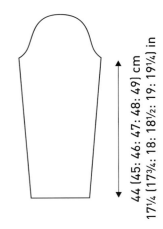

44 (45: 46: 47: 48: 49) cm
17¼ (17¾: 18: 18½: 19: 19¼) in

DOLORES
SOFT ELEGANT SHRUG

Recommendation
Suitable for the knitter with a little experience
Please see page 11 for photograph.

	XS	S	M	L	XL	XXL	
To fit	**81**	**86**	**91**	**97**	**102**	**109**	cm
bust	32	34	36	38	40	43	in

Rowan Kidsilk Aura

| 7 | 7 | 8 | 8 | 9 | 10 | x 25gm |

Photographed in Pumice

Needles
1 pair 3¾mm (no 9) (US 5) needles
1 pair 4½mm (no 7) (US 7) needles
1 pair 5½mm (no 5) (US 9) needles

Tension
15 sts and 20 rows to 10 cm measured over
stocking stitch using 5½mm (US 9) needles.
21 sts and 29 rows to 10 cm measured over
stocking stitch using 3¾mm (US 5) needles.

Special abbreviations
MP = make picot as folls: cast on 1 st, cast off
1 st – one st on right needle.

BODY
Right front
Cast on 2 sts using 5½mm (US 9) needles.
Beg with a K row, work in st st as folls:
Work 1 row, ending with a RS row.
Now shape front opening edge and side
seam as folls:
Inc 1 st at end (front opening edge) of next
row and at same edge of foll 7 (9: 11: 13:
15: 19) rows, then on foll 6 (5: 5: 4: 4: 3) alt
rows, then on foll 4th row and **at same time**
inc 1 st at beg (side seam edge) of 2nd and
foll 11 (11: 12: 12: 13: 14) alt rows.
29 (30: 33: 34: 37: 41) sts.
Inc 1 st at side seam edge **only** on 2nd and
foll 2 (2: 3: 3: 2: 1) alt rows, then on foll 24
(24: 22: 22: 22: 22) rows, ending with a **RS**
row. 56 (57: 59: 60: 62: 65) sts.
Place marker at end of last row to denote
base of armhole opening.
Work 25 (27: 27: 29: 31: 33) rows, ending
with a WS row.**

Cast on 4 sts at beg of next row.
60 (61: 63: 64: 66: 69) sts.
Work 1 row.
Break yarn and leave sts on a holder.

Left front
Work as given for right front to **, reversing
shapings.
Work 1 row.
Cast on 4 sts at beg of next row.
60 (61: 63: 64: 66: 69) sts.

Join sections and shape back
Next row (RS): K across 60 (61: 63: 64:
66: 69) sts of left front, turn and cast on
22 (24: 24: 26: 26: 26) sts (for back neck),
turn and K across 60 (61: 63: 64: 66: 69)
sts of right front.
142 (146: 150: 154: 158: 164) sts.
Work 23 (25: 25: 27: 29: 31) rows, ending
with a WS row.
Place markers at both ends of last row to
denote base of armhole openings.

Dec 1 st at each end of next 25 (25: 23: 23:
23: 23) rows, then on foll 14 (14: 16: 16: 16:
16) alt rows.
64 (68: 72: 76: 80: 86) sts.
Work 1 row, ending with a WS row.
Cast off.

SLEEVES (both alike - worked downwards)
With RS facing and using 3¾mm (US 5)
needles, pick up and knit 54 (58: 58: 64: 68:
72) sts evenly along armhole opening row-end
edge between markers.
Beg with a P row, work in st st, shaping
sides by dec 1 st at each end of 6th (4th:
6th: 4th: 4th: 4th) and every foll 6th (6th:
6th: 6th: 4th: 4th) row to 38 (40: 46: 44:
62: 66) sts, then on every foll – (-: 8th: -:
6th: 6th) row until - (-: 42: -: 46: 48)
sts rem.
Work 7 (5: 7: 5: 5: 5) rows, ending with
a WS row.
Cast off **loosely.**

MAKING UP
Pin the pieces out and steam gently without
allowing the iron to touch the yarn.
Join side and sleeve seams using back stitch
or mattress stitch if preferred.

Front and hem band
Cast on 13 sts using 4½mm (US 7) needles.
Row 1 (WS): MP, K to end.
Row 2: Purl.
Row 3: MP, P to end.
Row 4: Knit.
These 4 rows form patt.
Cont in patt until strip, beg and ending at
base of right side seam, fits neatly up entire
right front opening edge, across back neck,
down entire left front opening edge, then
across back cast-off edge, ending after patt
row 4 and with a WS row.
Cast off.
Join cast-on and cast-off ends of strip.
Neatly sew front and hem band strip in place.

94.5 (97.5: 100: 102.5: 108: 109) cm
37 (38½: 39½: 40: 40½: 42½: 43) in

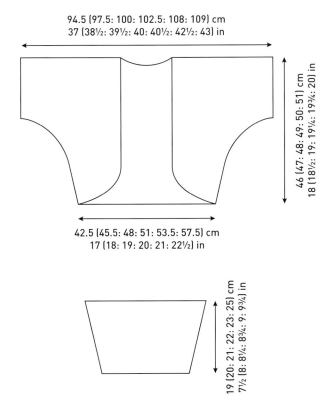

46 (47: 48: 49: 50: 51) cm
18 (18½: 19: 19¼: 19¾: 20) in

42.5 (45.5: 48: 51: 53.5: 57.5) cm
17 (18: 19: 20: 21: 22½) in

19 (20: 21: 22: 23: 25) cm
7½ (8: 8¼: 8¾: 9: 9¾) in

RUTH

Recommendation

Suitable for the knitter with a little experience
Please see page 35 for photograph.

	XS	S	M	L	XL	XXL	
To fit	**81**	**86**	**91**	**97**	**102**	**109**	cm
bust	32	34	36	38	40	43	in

Rowan Baby Alpaca DK

| | 9 | 9 | 10 | 10 | 11 | 11 | x 50gm |

Photographed in Southdown

Needles

1 pair 2¾mm (no 12) (US 2) needles
1 pair 3mm (no 11) (US 2/3) needles
1 pair 3¼mm (no 10) (US 3) needles
Cable needle

Buttons - 10

Tension

27½ sts and 32 rows to 10 cm measured over
pattern using 3¼mm (US 3) needles.

Special abbreviations

C4B = slip next 2 sts onto cable needle and
leave at back of work, K2, then K2 from cable
needle;
C4F = slip next 2 sts onto cable needle and
leave at front of work, K2, then K2 from cable
needle.

BACK and FRONT (both alike)

Cast on 97 (103: 109: 115: 123: 129) sts
using 3mm (US 2/3) needles.
Row 1 (RS): P1 (0: 1: 0: 0: 1), (K1 tbl, P1) 1
(3: 0: 2: 4: 1) times, K1, inc in next st, K1, *P1,
(K1 tbl, P1) twice, K1, inc in next st, K1, *P1,
(K1 tbl, P1) twice, K1, inc in next st, K1, rep
from * to last 3 (6: 1: 4: 8: 3) sts, (P1, K1 tbl)
1 (3: 0: 2: 4: 1) times, P1 (0: 1: 0: 0: 1). 109
(115: 123: 129: 137: 145) sts.
Row 2: K1 (0: 1: 0: 0: 1), (P1, K1) 1 (3: 0: 2:
4: 1) times, P4, *K1, (P1, K1) twice, P4, rep
from * to last 3 (6: 1: 4: 8: 3) sts, (K1, P1) 1
(3: 0: 2: 4: 1) times, K1 (0: 1: 0: 0: 1).
Row 3: P1 (0: 1: 0: 0: 1), (K1 tbl, P1) 1 (3: 0:
2: 4: 1) times, K4, *P1, (K1 tbl, P1) twice, K4,
rep from * to last 3 (6: 1: 4: 8: 3) sts, (P1, K1
tbl) 1 (3: 0: 2: 4: 1) times, P1 (0: 1: 0: 0: 1).
Rows 4 and 5: As rows 2 and 3.
Row 6: As row 4.
Row 7: P1 (0: 1: 0: 0: 1), (K1 tbl, P1) 1 (3:
0: 2: 4: 1) times, C4B, *P1, (K1 tbl, P1) twice,
C4B, rep from * 4 (4: 5: 5: 5: 6) times more,
**P1, (K1 tbl, P1) twice, C4F, rep from ** to
last 3 (6: 1: 4: 8: 3) sts, (P1, K1 tbl) 1 (3: 0:
2: 4: 1) times, P1 (0: 1: 0: 0: 1).
Rows 8 to 15: As rows 2 and 3, 4 times.
Row 16: As row 2.
Change to 3¼mm (US 3) needles.
Now work in patt as folls:
Row 1 (RS): Inc in first st, P2 (5: 0: 3: 7: 2),
C4B, *P5, C4B, rep from * 4 (4: 5: 5: 5: 6)
times more, **P5, C4F, rep from ** to last 3 (6:
1: 4: 8: 3) sts, P2 (5: 0: 3: 7: 2), inc in last st.
111 (117: 125: 131: 139: 147) sts.
Row 2: K4 (7: 2: 5: 9: 4), P4, *K5, P4, rep
from * to last 5 (7: 2: 5: 9: 4) sts, K4 (7: 2: 5: 9: 4).
Row 3: P4 (7: 2: 5: 9: 4), K4, *P5, K4, rep
from * to last 5 (7: 2: 5: 9: 4) sts, P4 (7: 2: 5:
9: 4).
Rows 4 to 9: As rows 2 and 3, 3 times.
Row 10: As row 2.
These 10 rows form patt and beg side seam
shaping.
Cont in patt, shaping side seams by inc
1 st at each end of next and foll 10th row,
then on 2 foll 12th rows, taking inc sts into
rev st st.
119 (125: 133: 139: 147: 155) sts.
Cont straight until work measures 23 (23: 24:
24: 24: 24) cm, ending with a WS row.

Shape armholes

Keeping patt correct, cast off 4 (5: 5: 6: 6: 7)
sts at beg of next 2 rows.
111 (115: 123: 127: 135: 141) sts.
Dec 1 st at each end of next 7 (7: 9: 9: 11:
11) rows, then on foll 2 (3: 3: 4: 4: 6) alt rows,
then on 2 foll 4th rows.
89 (91: 95: 97: 101: 103) sts.
Cont straight until armhole measures 15 (16:
16: 17: 18: 19) cm, ending with a WS row.

Shape neck

Next row (RS): Patt 21 (21: 23: 23:
25: 26) sts and turn, leaving rem sts
on a holder.
Work each side of neck separately.
Keeping patt correct, dec 1 st at neck edge
of next 9 rows, ending with a WS row.
12 (12: 14: 14: 16: 17) sts.

Shape shoulder

Cast off 4 (4: 4: 4: 5: 5) sts at beg and dec
1 st at end of next row.
Work 1 row.
Cast off 4 (4: 4: 4: 5: 5) sts at beg of next row.
Work 1 row.
Cast off rem 3 (3: 5: 5: 5: 6) sts.
With RS facing, rejoin yarn to rem sts, cast off
centre 47 (49: 49: 51: 51: 51) sts, patt to end.
(**Note:** When casting off across top of cables,
work "K1, K2tog, K1" to dec 1 st.)
Complete to match first side, reversing
shapings.

LEFT SLEEVE

Front sleeve

Cast on 35 (36: 36: 38: 39: 40) sts using
3mm (US 2/3) needles.
Row 1 (RS): *P1, (K1 tbl, P1) twice, K1, inc in
next st, K1, rep from * to last 3 (4: 4: 6: 7: 0)
sts, (P1, K1 tbl) 1 (2: 2: 2: 2: 0) times, P1 (0:
0: 1: 1: 0), K0 (0: 0: 1: 2: 0).
39 (40: 40: 42: 43: 45) sts.
Row 2: P0 (0: 0: 1: 2: 0), K1 (0: 0: 1: 1: 0),
(P1, K1) 1 (2: 2: 2: 2: 0) times, *P4, (K1, P1)
twice, K1, rep from * to end.
Row 3: *P1, (K1 tbl, P1) twice, K4, rep from *
to last 3 (4: 4: 6: 7: 0) sts, (P1, K1 tbl) 1 (2: 2:
2: 2: 0) times, P1 (0: 0: 1: 1: 0), K0 (0: 0: 1:
2: 0).
Rows 4 and 5: As rows 2 and 3.
Row 6: As row 2.

Row 7: P1, (K1 tbl, P1) twice, C4B, *P1, (K1 tbl, P1) twice, C4F, rep from * to last 3 (4: 4: 6: 7: 9) sts, (P1, K1 tbl) 1 (2: 2: 2: 2: 2) times, P1 (0: 0: 1: 1: 1), K0 (0: 0: 1: 2: 4).
Rows 8 and 9: As rows 2 and 3.
Row 10: As row 2.
These 10 rows form fancy rib.
Change to 3¼mm (US 3) needles.
Cont in fancy rib, inc 1 st at end of next and 2 foll 8th rows, taking inc sts into patt. 42 (43: 43: 45: 46: 48) sts.
Work 5 rows, ending with a WS row.
Break yarn and leave sts on a holder.

Back sleeve
Cast on 19 (20: 20: 22: 23: 24) sts using 3mm (US 2/3) needles.
Row 1 (RS): K0 (0: 0: 1: 2: 0), P1 (0: 0: 1: 1: 0), (K1 tbl, P1) 1 (2: 2: 2: 2: 0) times, *K1, inc in next st, K1, (P1, K1 tbl) twice, P1, rep from * to end.
21 (22: 22: 24: 25: 27) sts.
Row 2: *K1, (P1, K1) twice, P4, rep from * to last 3 (4: 4: 6: 7: 0) sts, (K1, P1) 1 (2: 2: 2: 2: 0) times, K1 (0: 0: 1: 1: 0), P0 (0: 0: 1: 2: 0).
Row 3: K0 (0: 0: 1: 2: 0), P1 (0: 0: 1: 1: 0), (K1 tbl, P1) 1 (2: 2: 2: 2: 0) times, *K4, (P1, K1 tbl) twice, P1, rep from * to end.
Rows 4 and 5: As rows 2 and 3.
Row 6: As row 2.
Row 7: K0 (0: 0: 1: 2: 4), P1 (0: 0: 1: 1: 1), (K1 tbl, P1) 1 (2: 2: 2: 2: 2) times, *C4B, (P1, K1 tbl) twice, P1, rep from * to end.
Rows 8 and 9: As rows 2 and 3.
Row 10: As row 2.
These 10 rows form fancy rib.
Change to 3¼mm (US 3) needles.
Cont in fancy rib, inc 1 st at beg of next and 2 foll 8th rows, taking inc sts into patt. 24 (25: 25: 27: 28: 30) sts.
Work 5 rows, ending with a WS row.

Join sections
Next row (RS): P0 (0: 0: 0: 1: 3), K1 (2: 2: 4: 4: 4), (P5, K4) twice, holding WS of sleeve front against RS of sleeve back, P tog first st of sleeve front with next st of sleeve back, (P tog next st of sleeve front with next st of sleeve back) 4 times, (K4, P5) 4 times, K1 (2: 2: 4: 4: 4), P0 (0: 0: 0: 1: 3).
61 (63: 63: 67: 69: 73) sts.
***Now work in patt as folls:
Row 1 (WS): K0 (0: 0: 0: 1: 3), P1 (2: 2: 4: 4: 4), *K5, P4, rep from * to last 6 (7: 7: 0: 1: 3) sts, K5 (5: 5: 0: 1: 3), P1 (2: 2: 0: 0: 0).
Row 2: Inc in first st, P0 (0: 0: 0: 0: 2), K0 (1: 1: 3: 4: 4), *P5, K4, rep from * to last 6 (7: 7: 9: 1: 3) sts, P5 (5: 5: 5: 0: 2), K0 (1: 1: 3: 0: 0), inc in last st. 63 (65: 65: 69: 71: 75) sts.

Row 3: K0 (0: 0: 1: 2: 4), P2 (3: 3: 4: 4: 4), *K5, P4, rep from * to last 7 (8: 8: 1: 2: 4) sts, K5 (5: 5: 1: 2: 4), P2 (3: 3: 0: 0: 0).
Row 4: P0 (0: 0: 1: 2: 4), K2 (3: 3: 0: 0: 0), (C4B) 0 (0: 0: 1: 1: 1) times, (P5, C4B) 3 times, (P5, C4F) 3 (3: 3: 4: 4: 4) times, P5 (5: 5: 1: 2: 4), K2 (3: 3: 0: 0: 0).
Row 5: As row 3.
Row 6: P0 (0: 0: 1: 2: 4), K2 (3: 3: 4: 4: 4), *P5, K4, rep from * to last 7 (8: 8: 1: 2: 4) sts, P5 (5: 5: 1: 2: 4), K2 (3: 3: 0: 0: 0).
Row 7: As row 3.
Row 8: As row 6.
Row 9: As row 3.
Row 10: Inc in first st, P0 (0: 0: 0: 1: 3), K1 (2: 2: 4: 4: 4), *P5, K4, rep from * to last 7 (8: 8: 1: 2: 4) sts, P5 (5: 5: 0: 1: 3), K1 (2: 2: 0: 0: 0), inc in last st.
65 (67: 67: 71: 73: 77) sts.
These 10 rows form patt and cont sleeve shaping.
Cont in patt, shaping sides by inc 1 st at each end of 8th and 3 (6: 4: 3: 1: 0) foll 8th rows, then on every foll 10th row until there are 83 (87: 87: 91: 93: 97) sts, taking inc sts into patt.
Cont straight until sleeve measures 44 (45: 46: 47: 48: 49) cm, ending with a WS row.

Shape top
Keeping patt correct, cast off 4 (5: 5: 6: 6: 7) sts at beg of next 2 rows.
75 (77: 77: 79: 81: 83) sts.
Dec 1 st at each end of next 3 rows, then on foll alt row, then on 7 foll 4th rows.
53 (55: 55: 57: 59: 61) sts.
Work 1 row, ending with a WS row.
Dec 1 st at each end of next and every foll alt row to 49 sts, then on foll 5 rows, ending with a WS row.
Cast off rem 39 sts.
(**Note:** When casting off across top of cables, work "K1, K2tog, K1" to dec 1 st.)

RIGHT SLEEVE
Back sleeve
Cast on 19 (20: 20: 22: 23: 24) sts using 3mm (US 2/3) needles.
Row 1 (RS): *(P1, K1 tbl) twice, P1, K1, inc in next st, K1, rep from * to last 3 (4: 4: 6: 7: 0) sts, (P1, K1 tbl) 1 (2: 2: 2: 2: 0) times, P1 (0: 0: 1: 1: 0), K0 (0: 0: 1: 2: 0).
21 (22: 22: 24: 25: 27) sts.
Row 2: P0 (0: 0: 1: 2: 0), K1 (0: 0: 1: 1: 0), (P1, K1) 1 (2: 2: 2: 2: 0) times, *P4, K1, (P1, K1) twice, rep from * to end.

Row 3: *(P1, K1 tbl) twice, P1, K4, rep from * to last 3 (4: 4: 6: 7: 0) sts, (P1, K1 tbl) 1 (2: 2: 2: 2: 0) times, P1 (0: 0: 1: 1: 0), K0 (0: 0: 1: 2: 0).
Rows 4 and 5: As rows 2 and 3.
Row 6: As row 2.
Row 7: *(P1, K1 tbl) twice, P1, C4F, rep from * to last 3 (4: 4: 6: 7: 9) sts, (P1, K1 tbl) 1 (2: 2: 2: 2: 2) times, P1 (0: 0: 1: 1: 1), K0 (0: 0: 1: 2: 4).
Rows 8 and 9: As rows 2 and 3.
Row 10: As row 2.
These 10 rows form fancy rib.
Change to 3¼mm (US 3) needles.
Cont in fancy rib, inc 1 st at end of next and 2 foll 8th rows, taking inc sts into patt. 24 (25: 25: 27: 28: 30) sts.
Work 5 rows, ending with a WS row.
Break yarn and leave sts on a holder.

Front sleeve
Cast on 35 (36: 36: 38: 39: 40) sts using 3mm (US 2/3) needles.
Row 1 (RS): K0 (0: 0: 1: 2: 0), P1 (0: 0: 1: 1: 0), (K1 tbl, P1) 1 (2: 2: 2: 2: 0) times, *K1, inc in next st, K1, P1, (K1 tbl, P1) twice, rep from * to end.
39 (40: 40: 42: 43: 45) sts.
Row 2: *(K1, P1) twice, K1, P4, rep from * to last 3 (4: 4: 6: 7: 0) sts, (K1, P1) 1 (2: 2: 2: 2: 0) times, K1 (0: 0: 1: 1: 0), P0 (0: 0: 1: 2: 0).
Row 3: K0 (0: 0: 1: 2: 0), P1 (0: 0: 1: 1: 0), (K1 tbl, P1) 1 (2: 2: 2: 2: 0) times, *K4, P1, (K1 tbl, P1) twice, rep from * to end.
Rows 4 and 5: As rows 2 and 3.
Row 6: As row 2.
Row 7: K0 (0: 0: 1: 2: 4), P1 (0: 0: 1: 1: 1), (K1 tbl, P1) 1 (2: 2: 2: 2: 2) times, *C4B, P1, (K1 tbl, P1) twice, rep from * to last 9 sts, C4F, P1, (K1 tbl, P1) twice.
Rows 8 and 9: As rows 2 and 3.
Row 10: As row 2.
These 10 rows form fancy rib.
Change to 3¼mm (US 3) needles.
Cont in fancy rib, inc 1 st at beg of next and 2 foll 8th rows, taking inc sts into patt. 42 (43: 43: 45: 46: 48) sts.
Work 5 rows, ending with a WS row.

Join sections
Next row (RS): P0 (0: 0: 0: 1: 3), K1 (2: 2: 4: 4: 4), (P5, K4) 4 times, holding WS of sleeve front against RS of sleeve back, P tog first st of sleeve front with next st of sleeve back, (P tog next st of sleeve front with next st of sleeve back) 4 times, (K4, P5) twice, K1 (2: 2: 4: 4: 4), P0 (0: 0: 0: 1: 3).
61 (63: 63: 67: 69: 73) sts.
Complete as given for left sleeve from ***.

MAKING UP

Pin the pieces out and steam gently without allowing the iron to touch the yarn.

Join right shoulder seam using back stitch or mattress stitch if preferred.

Neckband

With RS facing and using 2¾mm (US 2) needles, pick up and knit 12 sts down left side of front neck, 42 (44: 44: 46: 46: 46) sts from front, 12 sts up right side of front neck, 12 sts down right side of back neck, 42 (44: 44: 46: 46: 46) sts from back, then 12 sts up left side of back neck. 132 (136: 136: 140: 140: 140) sts.

Beg with a K row, work in rev st st for 4 rows, ending with a **RS** row.

Cast off knitwise (on **WS**).

Join left shoulder and neckband seam. Join side seams. Join sleeve seams. Insert sleeves into armholes. Sew on buttons, attaching 5 buttons to each cuff through edges of both sleeve front and back as in photograph.

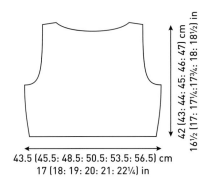

43.5 (45.5: 48.5: 50.5: 53.5: 56.5) cm
17 (18: 19: 20: 21: 22¼) in

42 (43: 44: 45: 46: 47) cm
16½ (17: 17¼:17¾: 18: 18½) in

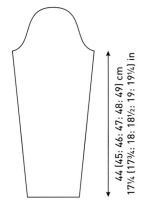

44 (45: 46: 47: 48: 49) cm
17¼ (17¾: 18: 18½: 19: 19¼) in

Recommendation

Suitable for the knitter with a little experience
Please see pages 29, 45 & 46 for photographs.

One size

Rowan Kid Classic

8   x 50gm
Photographed in Smoke

Needles

1 pair 4½mm (no 7) (US 7) needles
Cable needle

Tension

21 sts and 27 rows to 10 cm measured over
stocking stitch using 4½mm (US 7) needles.

Finished size

Completed scarf is approx 30 cm (12 in) wide
and 250 cm (98½ in) long.

Special abbreviations

MP = make picot as folls: cast on 1 st, cast off
1 st – one st on right needle;
C4B = slip next 2 sts onto cn and leave at
back of work, K2, then K2 from cn;
C6B = slip next 3 sts onto cn and leave at
back of work, K3, then K3 from cn;
C8B = slip next 4 sts onto cn and leave at
back of work, K4, then K4 from cn.

BOBBY
LONG-LINE CABLED SCARF

SCARF

Cast on 75 sts using 4½mm (US 7) needles.
Row 1 (RS): MP, K until there are 9 sts on right
needle, P5, K6, (P1, K1) 3 times, P1, K8, (P1, K1)
3 times, P1, K6, P5, K6, (P1, K1) twice, P1, K11.
Row 2: MP, K until there are 5 sts on right
needle, P6, (P1, K1) twice, P7, K5, P6, (P1, K1)
3 times, P9, (P1, K1) 3 times, P7, K5, P4, K5.
Row 3: K9, P5, K6, (P1, K1) 3 times, P1, K8,
(P1, K1) 3 times, P1, K6, P5, K6, (P1, K1)
twice, P1, K11.
Row 4: K5, P6, (P1, K1) twice, P7, K5, P6, (P1, K1)
3 times, P9, (P1, K1) 3 times, P7, K5, P4, K5.
Rows 5 to 20: As rows 1 to 4, 4 times.
Row 21: MP, K until there are 5 sts on right
needle, C4B, P5, K6, (P1, K1) 3 times, P1, K8,
(P1, K1) 3 times, P1, C6B, P5, K6, (P1, K1)
twice, P1, K11.
Rows 22 to 24: As rows 2 to 4.
Rows 25 to 28: As rows 1 to 4.
Rows 29 and 30: As rows 1 and 2.
Row 31: K5, C4B, P5, K6, (P1, K1) 3 times,
P1, C8B, (P1, K1) 3 times, P1, K6, P5, C6B,
(P1, K1) twice, P1, K11.
Row 32: As row 4.
Rows 33 to 40: As rows 1 to 4, twice.
Row 41: MP, K until there are 5 sts on right
needle, C4B, P5, C6B, (P1, K1) 3 times, P1,
K8, (P1, K1) 3 times, P1, C6B, P5, K6, (P1, K1)
twice, P1, C6B, K5.
Rows 42 to 44: As rows 2 to 4.
Rows 45 to 48: As rows 1 to 4.
Rep rows 29 to 48, 30 times more, then rows
29 to 40 again.
Next row (RS): As row 21.
Rep rows 2 to 4 once more.
Now rep rows 1 to 4, 4 times, ending with
a WS row.
Cast off.

INFORMATION

A GUIDE TO ASSIST WITH TECHNIQUES & FINISHING TOUCHES

TENSION

Achieving the correct tension has to be one of the most important elements in producing a beautiful, well fitting knitted garment. The tension controls the size and shape of your finished piece and any variation to either stitches or rows, however slight, will affect your work and change the fit completely.
To avoid any disappointment, we would always recommend that you knit a tension square in the yarn and stitch given in the pattern, working perhaps four or five more stitches and rows than those given in the tension note.

When counting the tension, place your knitting on a flat surface and mark out a 10cm square with pins. Count the stitches between the pins. If you have too many stitches to 10cm your knitting it too tight, try again using thicker needles, if you have too few stitches to 10cm your knitting is too loose, so try again using finer needles. Please note, if you are unable to achieve the correct stitches and rows required, the stitches are more crucial as many patterns are knitted to length.
Keep an eye on your tension during knitting, especially if you're going back to work which has been put to one side for any length of time.

SIZING

The instructions are given for the smallest size. Where they vary, work the figures in brackets for the larger sizes. One set of figures refers to all sizes. The size diagram with each pattern will help you decide which size to knit. The measurements given on the size diagram are the actual size your garment should be when completed.
Measurements will vary from design to design because the necessary ease allowances have been made in each pattern to give your garment the correct fit, i.e. a loose fitting

garment will be several cm wider than a neat fitted one, a snug fitting garment may have no ease at all.

WRAP STITCH

A wrap stitch is used to eliminate the hole created when using the short row shaping method. Work to the position on the row indicated in the pattern, wrap the next st (by slipping next st onto right needle, taking yarn to opposite side of work between needles and then slipping same st back onto left needle – on foll rows, K tog the loop and the wrapped st) and turn, cont from pattern.

CHART NOTE

Some of our patterns include a chart. Each square on a chart represent a stitch and each line of squares a row of knitting.

When working from a chart, unless otherwise stated, read odd rows (RS) from right to left and even rows (WS) from left to right. The key alongside each chart indicates how each stitch is worked.

INTARSIA TECHNIQUE

The intarsia method of knitting produces a single thickness of fabric and is used where a colour is only required in a particular area of a row. Use short lengths of yarn for each block of colour, then joining in the different colours at the appropriate point on the row, link one colour to the next by twisting them around each other where they meet on the wrong side to avoid gaps. Ends can then be darned along the colour join lines, as each motif is completed.

FINISHING INSTRUCTIONS

It is the pressing and finishing which will transform your knitted pieces into a garment to be proud of.

Pressing

Darn in ends neatly along the selvage edge. Follow closely any special instructions given on the pattern or ball band and always take great care not to over press your work.
Block out your knitting on a pressing or ironing board, easing into shape, and unless otherwise states, press each piece using a warm iron over a damp cloth.

Tip: Attention should be given to ribs/edgings; if the garment is close fitting – steam the ribs gently so that the stitches fill out but stay elastic. Alternatively if the garment is to hang straight then steam out to the correct shape.

Tip: Take special care to press the selvages, as this will make sewing up both easier and neater.

CONSTRUCTION
Stitching together

When stitching the pieces together, remember to match areas of pattern very carefully where they meet. Use a stitch such as back stitch or mattress stitch for all main knitting seams and join all ribs and neckband with mattress stitch, unless otherwise stated.
Take extra care when stitching the edgings and collars around the back neck of a garment. They control the width of the back neck, and if too wide the garment will be ill fitting and drop off the shoulder.
Knit back neck edgings only to the length stated in the pattern, even stretching it slightly if for example, you are working in garter or horizontal rib stitch.
Stitch edgings/collars firmly into place using a back stitch seam, easing-in the back neck to fit the collar/edging rather than stretching the collar/edging to fit the back neck.

Set-in sleeves: Join side and sleeve seams. Place centre of cast off edge of sleeve to shoulder seams. Set in sleeve, easing sleeve head into armhole.

CARE INSTRUCTIONS

Yarns
Follow the care instructions printed on each individual ball band. Where different yarns are used in the same garment, follow the care instructions for the more delicate one.

Buttons
We recommend that buttons are removed if your garment is to be machine washed.

CROCHET
We are aware that crochet terminology varies from country to country. Please note we have used the English style in this publication.

CROCHET
We are aware that crochet terminology varies from country to country. Please note we have used the English style in this publication.

Crochet abbreviations

ch	chain
ss	slip stitch
dc	double crochet
htr	half treble
tr	treble
dtr	double treble
yoh	yarn over hook
sp(s)	space(s)

Double crochet
1 Insert the hook into the work (as indicated in the pattern), wrap the yarn over the hook and draw the yarn through the work only.
2 Wrap the yarn again and draw the yarn through both loops on the hook.
3 1 dc made

ABBREVIATIONS

K	knit
P	purl
K1b	knit 1 through back loop
st(s)	stitch(es)
inc	increas(e)(ing)
dec	decreas(e)(ing)
st st	stocking stitch (1 row K, 1 row P)
garter st	garter stitch (K every row)
beg	begin(ning)
foll	following
rem	remain(ing)
rev st st	reverse stocking stitch (1 row P, 1 row K)
rep	repeat
alt	alternate
cont	continue
patt	pattern
tog	together
mm	millimetres
cm	centimetres
in(s)	inch(es)
RS	right side
WS	wrong side
sl 1	slip one stitch
psso	pass slipped stitch over
tbl	through back of loop
M1	make one stitch by picking up horizontal loop before next stitch and knitting into back of it
M1p	make one stitch by picking up horizontal loop before next stitch and purling into back of it
yfwd	yarn forward
yon	yarn over needle
yrn	yarn round needle
MP	Make picot: Cast on 1 st, by inserting the right needle between the first and second stitch on left needle, take yarn round needle, bring loop through and place on left (one stitch cast on), cast off 1 st, by knitting first the loop and then the next stitch, pass the first stitch over the second (one stitch cast off).
Cn	cable needle
C4B	Cable 4 back: Slip next 2 sts onto a cn and hold at back of work, K2, K2 from cn.
C4F	Cable 4 front: Slip next 2 sts onto a cn and hold at front of work, K2, K2 from cn.

THANK YOU...

We would like to express our appreciation to our incredible team. Firstly to Graham for the wonderful photographs and editorial design, Angela for her skills on the page layouts, our fabulous models Amanda and James, and Diana for her hair & make-up talents, Sue Whiting and Tricia for their pattern writing & checking expertise, the lovely Ann for all the yarn support, Ella, Sandra, Arna, Betty, Joan, Mary, Margaret and Glennis for their beautiful knitting, and to Susan for finishing the garments so well.

Our gratitude also goes to Philip, Rita, June and all at Lydgate Chapel and Kevin, Peter, Sara and all at Cliffe House www.cliffehouse.co.uk for allowing us to shoot at the fantastic locations, Clifford for the loan of his motorbike, Helene at Revival www.revivalvintage.co.uk, and the team at Be Authentic www.b-authentic.co.uk

Thanks to you all for making another book possible.

Kim, Kathleen and Lindsay

INDEX